Taking to the Air

Taking to the Air

An Illustrated History of Flight

Lily Ford

First published in 2018 by
The British Library
96 Euston Road
London NW1 2DB

Text © Lily Ford 2018
All images © British Library Board and
other named copyright holders 2018

ISBN 978 0 7123 5261 1

Cataloguing in Publication Data
A catalogue record for this publication is available
from the British Library

Designed by Chris Benfield
Picture research by Sally Nicholls
Printed and bound in China by
C&C Offset Printing

COVER: Board from a French game, 'Une expedition
aérienne: jeu instrutif et amusant pous la jeunesse',
1880–1910.

FRONTISPIECE: A vision by J. S. Pugh of balloon traffic
rendering the Panama Canal obsolete. From *Puck*
magazine, 31 January 1906.

Contents

Introduction

The possibilities of flight have long fascinated us. Myths and fantasies of taking to the air abound in classical, medieval and early modern literature. Each new advance in the sphere of aeronautics captivated a broad public, from those who gathered to witness winged medieval visionaries jumping from towers to those who tuned in to watch the moon landings. Crowds flocked to eighteenth-century balloon launches; early twentieth-century air shows attracted hundreds of thousands. The visibility of airborne objects from the ground makes for a democratic spectacle of flight, one open to both intentional and inadvertent viewing. Such objects cry out to be depicted, for their strangeness and their novel appearance in a familiar landscape.

Unlike most general works on aviation, this book approaches the history of flight through its spectators, and later on its passengers. It focuses on flight as popular entertainment, as spectacle, as something experienced by the great majority of people on the ground, not just those lucky enough to make it into the air. Many books have been written about famous inventors and aviators, and about the feats of design and engineering involved in aeronautics, both civil and military. A few address the cultural dimensions of flight, such as Robert Wohl's excellent pair of books on aviation and the Western imagination.[1] But to date the wealth of visual material dealing with the performance and spectacle of flight has not been exploited.

Taking to the Air is based on the large and diverse collection of print imagery held by the British Library, from medieval woodcut prototypes to Regency ballooning narratives, from photographic records of aircraft to Biggles. It tracks a much broader participation in flight, an imaginative, vicarious involvement on the part of readers and viewers. This focus does away with some of the traditional milestones and epochal and disciplinary divisions of aviation history. The chapters run in roughly chronological order, but they are themed around moments of cultural impact rather than technological progress. The book also attends to apparently trivial artefacts such as toys and makes a start at bringing women into the history of flight, which seems traditionally to have been told by men to men and boys.

Just as the chronological breadth of *Taking to the Air* is shaped by the nature of its source material, so is its geographical focus. Aviation is a profoundly national business, which is obvious not only in its twentieth-century development but also at the birth of ballooning in the 1780s and even before, with seventeenth-century royal courts retaining aeronautical engineers. As George Orwell remarked with exasperation in the face of the prevailing niceties about aeroplanes and radio making the world smaller, aviation has done more to reinforce borders than to erase them.[2] While the first three chapters of the book have a European bent, reviewing developments in countries such as France and Germany, the story of flight told here is a British one. This is not to ignore the international cross-currents of expertise and cultural forms feeding British development; it is simply a practical and pragmatic framing that recognizes the structural economic foundations of twentieth-century aviation. The emphasis on Britain, and on printed matter, gives the book a natural end point. In 1969 experts in flight technology had set their sights outside the earth's atmosphere and the antagonists of aerial nationalism were the United States and the Soviet Union. Humans had, at last, orbited the earth and landed on the moon. These new milestones were conveyed not so much in print, but rather through the audiovisual technologies of radio and television.

A history of flight this brief cannot hope to be comprehensive. But, by offering a new reading of the history of aviation that focuses on the imagined community of flight, it provides a context for the graphic responses pulled from the archive. Here the spectator and the consumer of pamphlets, newsreels and novels figures as prominently as flight's traditional protagonists. It is a study of how flight has been thought and pictured.

ABOVE: A De Havilland Gipsy Moth flies over an African river. In an illustration by Leslie Carr for the children's book *Motor and Plane* by Cyril Hall, 1932. PAGE 6: A De Havilland DH34 being loaded up for an Imperial Airways flight, cover of *Airways* magazine, 1 September 1926.

1   Winged Men

> The fate of Icarus frightened no one. Wings!
> wings! wings! they cried from all sides, even if we
> should fall into the sea. To fall from the sky, one
> must climb there, even for but a moment, and that
> is more beautiful than to spend one's whole life
> crawling on the earth.
> – Théophile Gautier, *Histoire du Romantisme* (1872)[3]

For forty seconds Franz Reichelt stands on the parapet of the Eiffel Tower. Gently shrugging his arms, he shakes out the folds of his wingsuit as he looks down over the edge. With its high, stiffened collar and cocoon shape, it resembles a funeral shroud more than a flight device. Surely Reichelt is contemplating his imminent death. But perhaps not – perhaps he is relishing this moment, a moment of sheer audacity, poised over this stately capital city, a crowd of onlookers below, about to achieve his life's most glorious goal of flight. The Pathé cameramen, who have played their part in encouraging Reichelt to make the first filmed trial of this parachute, designed for pilots ditching from their aeroplanes, are stationed at the first floor and bottom of the tower. Finally he crouches forward and drops out of the frame. Cut to the lower camera, which shows a 90-degree plummet ending in a puff of dust. The crowd rushes in. Reichelt's lifeless body is carried away. The crater it made is measured.

This footage from 1912 is still, naturally, horrifying. But it reminds us of the compelling spectacle that flight could provide long before the age of aerostatics and aeronautics. There is a long genealogy behind Franz Reichelt of men – and it was always men – jumping from towers in the hope and conviction that their flying aids would take them soaring over their spectators. Reichelt made a contract with a new medium, that of film, but the most reliable way of ensuring both recognition for the feat and immediate medical attention should it fail was to perform for a crowd.

ABOVE: Tethered griffins lift Alexander the Great, from *Le Livre et le vraye hystoire du bon roy Alexandre*, *c.*1420. OPPOSITE: King Kai Kawus ascends using eagles, from a Persian manuscript of the *Shāhnāma* of Firdausī, 1586. Note the bait both he and Alexander have fixed on top of their conveyances. PAGE 10: Franz Reichelt plummeting to his death, illustration from *Le Petit Journal*, 18 February 1912.

For all those early flight attempts we know about, how many more went unrecorded? The lucky ones were talked and sung of, their exploits written down, illustrated and eventually published. They exist in this history because they caught the imagination of onlookers and chroniclers, or because they made up part of the supernatural attributes of great rulers. Alexander the Great flew in a chariot pulled by griffins, dangling meat just ahead of the beasts to keep them moving. Around 1500 BCE King Kai Kawus had his chariot drawn by eagles.

The stories of flight that persisted were those that lent themselves to retelling. A central role is played by Daedalus and Icarus in the story written down by Ovid around 8 CE. Locked in a tower on the island of Crete, the father and son decide to escape by flying off the top. This is the founding fiction for flight as a technology, as a power that can be achieved through design and courage. Icarus's hubristic downfall is the reason for this myth's staying power, but the incidentals – that the brilliant Daedalus looked to nature and chose to base his flying technology on the wings and flapping action of birds, and that his design was successful – had a lasting effect on

DAEDALUS AND ICARUS.

ABOVE: Daedalus and Icarus, depicted in a woodcut by Albrecht Dürer, 1493.
OPPOSITE: Satan and his demons, from the 1688 edition of John Milton's
Paradise Lost.

subsequent attempts to take flight. For a millennium and a half, efforts to fly focused on wings, whether fixed as in a glider or made to flap as in an ornithopter.

Daedalus and his son were not the first tower jumpers. There are records of several others (though the records date from later than the *Metamorphoses*). The Chinese emperor Qin Shi Huang was said to have evaded capture by leaping from a tower with two reed mats around 2200 BCE. The father of King Lear, Bladud, put his talent for necromantic arts to fatal test when he jumped from the roof of a temple in Trinaventum, now London, in 852 BCE. Injury or death from such attempts was common, but perhaps the potential gains, whether escape or respect, outweighed the risks.

After the establishment of Christianity in much of Europe over the first few centuries of the Common Era, attempts to fly were condemned. An apocryphal Bible parable tells of Simon the magician who performed levitation in the Roman Forum in the second century, only to fall from mid-air after a Christian apostle prayed to God to stop him. Flight was associated with magic, with the supernatural, and with the desire to surpass our native abilities. It was a special subject of the Christian devil, who tempted even

Christ to try flying; Satan and his demons were frequently given bat wings to differentiate them from the feathered appendages of angels. Wings remained an important visual signifier, as they had been along with other animal parts in pre-Christian spiritual iconography. They were also an attribute of mystical power even when they were not depicted visually, as with angels in the non-representational Jewish and Muslim traditions of art.

The best-educated scholars, with most time at their disposal for learned contemplation, were religious men. It is indicative of the realms of acceptable enquiry within the thirteenth-century church that Thomas Aquinas was encouraged to meditate on how many angels might dance on a pinhead, while Roger Bacon was censured for thinking up an ornithopter. Medieval Islam was less restrictive as regards scientific experiment than medieval Christianity. The first attempt we know of in the Middle Ages took place in 852, when the philosopher and poet Abbas ibn Firnas, equipped with a wing-like parachute, leapt from the minaret of the Cordoban mosque in Andalusia. The failure of this attempt led him to work on a fixed-wing device which he assayed twenty-three years later in front of a summoned crowd. He glided some distance before landing and damaging his back, attributing this mishap to his lack of a tail. Over a century later there were two geographically separate attempts to fly using wings, possibly inspired by Ibn Firnas. In 1002 the renowned Arabic lexicographer Abu al-Jawhari jumped from the roof of a mosque in which he had been teaching in Nishapur, now northern Iran, and died. In 1029 a British monk, Eilmer, launched himself from the tower of Malmesbury Abbey in Somerset and broke both legs; he survived and, like Ibn Firnas, rued his failure to build a tail into his design. An attempt in Constantinople by an unnamed inventor (known in European aviation lore simply – and anachronistically – as 'the Saracen') to demonstrate flight to Emperor Manuel Komnenos in 1162 resulted in the death of the flier, who proved too heavy for his reinforced cloth parachute.

After these relatively few documented attempts around 1000, the impulse to fly seems once more to have abated for several centuries in Europe, oppressed by the prevailing Christian attitude that it was the work of the devil. It was the Italian Renaissance that reignited the desire to achieve flight, with advances in engineering sponsored by dukes and executed by typically polymath figures such as Leonardo da Vinci and the mathematics professor Giovan Battista Danti. The latter had, sensibly, trialled his design of wings fixed with an iron bar over a lake, but chose to introduce the device to the public during a large wedding celebration in

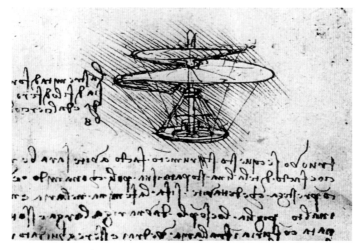

ABOVE: Airscrew design by Leonardo da Vinci, *c.*1500.
OVERLEAF: Fausto Veranzio (Faust Vrančić), 'Homo Volans',
from *Machinae Novae, c.*1615.

the middle of Perugia in 1503. He managed to swoop down over the heads
of a crowd gathered to watch jousting in the main square before crashing
into a church roof, but survived to continue teaching.

The potential for glory at the risk of public censure was not appealing
to Leonardo da Vinci. He knew well the volatile dynamic of public spectators. He had watched and possibly collaborated in the famous theatrical
pageants of 1470s Florence; the first sketches of wings in his extant papers
depict designs for the flying automata that featured in these shows. When
he did begin to work on a flying machine in the early 1490s, he procured
a large, closed attic in which to experiment with scale models. In spite of
the fact that Leonardo came up with the most compelling and evolved
mechanical designs for a man-powered flying machine for centuries, there
is no record of his demonstrating his prototypes in public. Perhaps he had
one eye on posterity, though his writings on aeronautics remained relatively unknown until they were removed from Italy by Napoleon in 1797.
The nearest he seems to have come to the spectacle of flight was making
phantasmagorical wax globes sputter irreverently around the courts of his
patrons. A century after Leonardo designed the first parachute, the Croa-
tian inventor Faust Vrančić (Fausto Veranzio) published a coincidentally
very similar prototype, Homo Volans, in a book of his own inventions.

38. HOMO VOLANS.

We have seen that professors and scholars were prepared to stake their dignity on the goal of flight. Danti was the first of several Italians across Europe to try their luck. In 1536 a clock-maker, Denis Bolori, leapt from the cathedral of Troyes in France, glided perhaps a mile and was killed on landing. Giovanni Damiano, or John Damian, secured a royal audience for his descent from the top of Stirling Castle in 1507. Damiano seems to have ended up in Scotland as the abbot of a local monastery after being hounded from other countries in Europe as a charlatan. James IV did not witness a very impressive flight; the injured abbot claimed that his eagle-wing plumage had been adulterated with chicken feathers. This followed the prevailing belief in a law of attraction, whereby chicken feathers are drawn to the ground (on which chickens live) while eagle feathers naturally rise to dwell in the upper air. The symbolic importance of an object was seen to be as effective as its proven material properties. An aspirant to flight in Portugal in 1540 hired the Viseu city herald to make known that a miracle would soon take place, in the form of a man flying with magic wings. While he used framed calico rather than feathers for the wings, he wore a beaked hood to evoke an eagle. The slipping of this hood caused him to crash into a rooftop and he died several days later.

The showmanship so often deployed in flight attempts also derived from existing practices. Complex mechanical devices emulated flight on stages across Europe from the fifteenth century onwards, and acrobatic stunt acts were well evolved. Tightrope walking was sometimes seen as analogous to flight. The Turkish chronicler Evliya Çelebi wrote that in mid-seventeenth-century Istanbul 'there are thirteen masters, each one capable of climbing to the sky on rope ladders and conversing with Jesus and the cherubim'.[4] By his account, two successful flights were made in the presence of Sultan Murad IV, by the ropewalkers Hezârfen Ahmed Çelebi and Lagari Hasan Çelebi. Hezârfen allegedly travelled two miles from the Galata Tower to the Asian side of Constantinople using a winged glider. Lagari launched himself on a giant rocket, using eagle feather wings to control his descent into the Bosphorus. Both were pensioned off by an impressed but discomfited sultan. Less successful was the French rope-walker Charles Allard, who, around 1660, suffered serious injuries when he attempted to fly from a tightrope in front of Louis XIV.

The seventeenth century marked a turning point for the theoretical approach to flight. The new climate of scientific investigation, in which Galileo Galilei, Johannes Kepler and René Descartes played significant roles, posed the most profound questions about the world in an empirical framework. Until this point there was a prevailing sense of flight as a divine mystery; only mavericks would presume to challenge the natural order of things by attempting ascension. Strong feelings still existed about the propriety of flight: 'What madness ... [to] attempt what God and Nature have forbid', exclaimed Thomas Heywood in 1635.[5] But in the seventeenth century attention to the mechanical and physical possibility of flight shifted from the sphere of religious contemplation to that of science, or natural philosophy. Almost all of the prominent theorists of flight at this time were religious, as it was impossible to advance in one's studies or to attend university without entering holy orders, but they regarded the subject of flight as a human endeavour rather than as trespassing on sacred ground. John Wilkins, bishop of Chester and warden of Wadham College, Oxford, was the first Briton since Roger Bacon in the thirteenth century to write positively and practically of flight in several scientific books of the 1630s and 1640s. It was his 1638 book *The Discovery of a World in the Moone*, speculating on the habitation of that body in acknowledgement of the recent astronomical discoveries by Galileo and Kepler, that had the greatest cultural impact. In *Mathematicall Magick* (1648) he set out the four ways in which flight had been or might be attempted: '1. By spirits, or angels. 2. By the help of fowls. 3. By wings fastened immediately to the body. 4. By a flying chariot.'[6] Wilkins's matter-of-fact listing of supernatural and natural elements together is a reminder of the intellectual climate of his time: he was ruling nothing out. Of the four, the flying chariot may well have seemed the least plausible.

In the same year an episcopal colleague, Francis Godwin, published the first flight novel, in which a Spanish adventurer harnesses wild swans to carry him to the moon. For the next 150 years or so the narratives of Wilkins and Godwin would influence a romantic and proto-science fiction approach to flight and its possibilities, in the work of Robert Paltock, Cyrano de Bergerac, Richard Owen Cambridge, Jean-Jacques Rousseau, Samuel Johnson and Restif de la Bretonne, among others.

It was no coincidence that Wilkins's and Godwin's books appeared only four years after the first translation into English of Lucian's *True History*. The second-century satirist told the stories of his own voyage to the moon and of Icaromenippus, a character who, after consulting many argumentative philosophers on how to fly, resolved to 'get me wings', and used one eagle wing and one vulture wing to transport himself to the moon. Lucian's techniques relied on the symbolic attributes of wings rather than

TOP: Plate from Francis Godwin, *The Man in the Moone*, 1638. BOTTOM: Detail from the frontispiece to *A true relation of the travels of M. Bush, a Gentleman* (1607), who built a pynace to take him from Lambourne, Berkshire to London. The vessel, launched from the church tower, was designed to travel 'threescore yards in the ayre, five and twentie miles upon the land, and an hundreth miles upon the water [sic]'.

ABOVE: Cyrano de Bergerac's *Voyage to the Sun*, frontispiece to the English edition of 1687. OPPOSITE: Using artificial wings, the hero Victorin elopes with his beloved Christine in Restif de la Bretonne's *Le Dédale Français*, 1781.

OVERLEAF (LEFT): Illustration by A. P. Garnett from *Lucian's Wonderland* by
St. J. B. W. Wilson, 1899. OVERLEAF (RIGHT): Design for Francesco Lana de Terzi's
flying machine, in *Novo metodo para poter viaggiare in aria*, 1784.

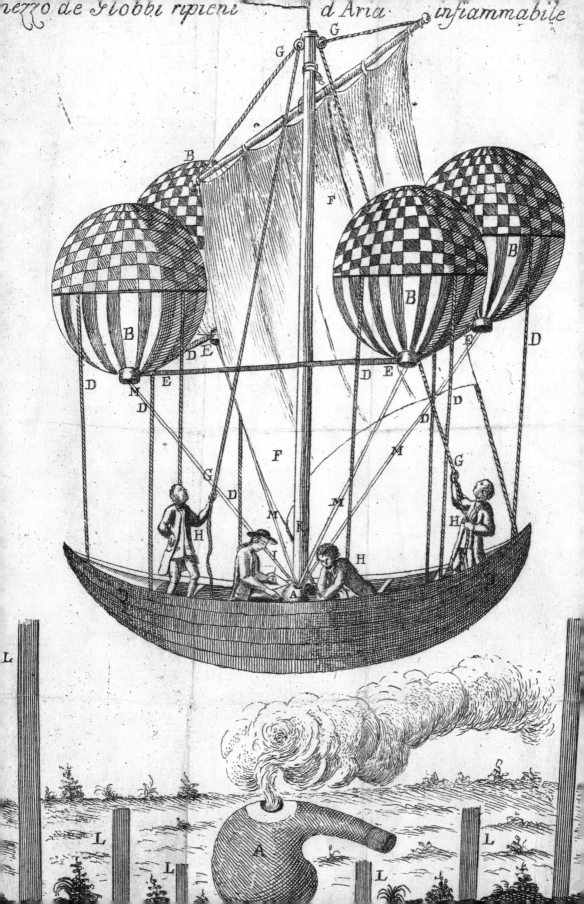

any physical logic, but read in a seventeenth-century context, they were not ridiculous. The use of symbols of flight and elevation in designs for flying apparatuses, regardless of how fit for purpose the designs were, suggests that encouraging belief in flight by association was as important as taking to the air.

Advances in physics, with the invention of the barometer and the air pump in the middle of the seventeenth century, led the European scientific community to consider the possibility of lighter-than-air flight. The Jesuit scholars Gaspar Schott, Athanasius Kircher and Francesco Lana de Terzi all published treatises suggesting that flying craft could be made to rise upwards by means of a vacuum. Lana de Terzi went so far as to build a model airship, though not to fly it. He reflected that God would surely never allow such a machine to be successful, since it 'would create many disturbances in the civil and political governments of mankind'.[7] In 1680 the mathematician Giovanni Alfonso Borelli concluded that flight could never be achieved by a man flapping wings, as he lacked the muscle power needed to move a large wing-span at speed. This did not stop tower jumpers; indeed the most momentous flight event of the century took place just a year or

ABOVE: Illustration of Besnier in Guillaume Louis Figuier's
Les Merveilles de Science, 1868. OPPOSITE: 'Chevalier Humgruffier and the Marquis de Gull making an excursion to the Moon in their new Aerial Vehicle', 1784.

so before Borelli published his treatise. A French locksmith, Besnier, had developed a glider operated by moving both arms and legs, and in the late 1670s he demonstrated it by crossing a river and travelling some distance from his town of Sablé, in the Maine region. By contrast with the patchy and shifting documentation of previous attempts, an account of Besnier's exploit appeared in no less than the *Journal des Savants*, from where it proceeded to make an impact on the scientific and wider community. Images of Besnier working his device, which resembled a crossed pair of oars, proliferated. Most of them represented him naked, in an Icarian state of grace. Having made his reputation, Besnier chose not to fly again and sold his oars to a travelling showman.

In Britain Robert Hooke received this news with great interest, translating into English this account of the flight, as well as Lana de Terzi's treatise. A friend and former student of John Wilkins, who made several attempts at testing Wilkins's ideas, Hooke claimed that he continued to experiment with flight over his lifetime. There is a suggestion that his interest in flight was also sustained by the elaborate stagecraft of London Restoration theatre, which often featured characters in flight.[8] Debates about flight, the means to achieve it and the resultant effect on society raged throughout the seventeenth century, and the theatre was not isolated from the climate of enquiry and sense of scientific discovery. For the first time the possibility of flight was considered outside the ivory tower, in coffee-houses and inns, in drawing rooms and public spaces. It provided grist to the mill of fantasists and satirists, and, as a stage upon which ancient and modern thinking were opposed, it played a role in Jonathan Swift's satire *The Battle of the Books* (1704).

Anyone could weigh in with an opinion, as long as he was a man. Dorothy Osborne recorded an incident in 1653 where she had been present during an after-dinner conversation with her brother and a male friend, who

> fell into a discourse of fflyeing, and both agreed that it was very possible to finde out a way that people might fly like Birds and dispatch their Journy's soe. I that had not said a word all night started up at that and desyr'd they would say a little more in it, for I had not marked the beginning, but instead of that they both fell into soe Violent a Laughing that I should appeare soe much concern'd in such an Art.[9]

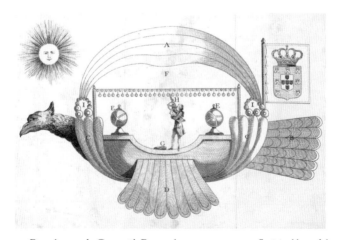

ABOVE: Bartolomeu de Gusmaõ's Passarola, 1709. OPPOSITE: Satirical broadsheet showing the uses to which Jean-Pierre Blanchard's Vaisseau Volant might be put, *c.*1782. PAGE 31: Jakob Degen's fall from grace, lavishly imagined by a French satirist as the 'Catastrophe of the Modern Dedalus'.

Embarquement d'un abbé
dans le Vaisseau volant.
Air? Vatan voir,
Au moindre chapeau vacant,
Maint abbé frivole,
S'en ira tout en planant,
Droit au Capitole.
Venez Pierre, venez Jean,
Voir comme il vole.

Embarquement d'un astrologue
dans le Vaisseau volant.
Air? Vatan voir,
L'Astrologue en parcourant,
l'Une et l'autre pôle;
Va des Cieux commodément,
Mirer la coupole.
Venez Pierre, venez Jean,
Voir comme il vole,

Débarquement de petits maîtres
dans le Vaisseau volant.
Air? Vatan voir,
J'en connois qui sur le champ,
Iron en cariole,
Aux Femmes du grand Sultan,
Parler gaudriole,
Venez Pierre, venez Jean,
Voir comme il vole;

Débarquement d'un soupirant
dans le Vaisseau volant.
Air? Vatan voir,
Pour moi, qui du sentiment,
Fais ma seule idole,
Je rabattrai constament,
Au pied de Nicole,
Va t'en voir s'il vole Jean,
Va t'en voir s'il vole,

It is perhaps not surprising to hear of guffaws at a woman expressing interest in scientific matters during this period. But the absence of women from the discourse of flight thus far is marked. Not a single winged woman appears in the many accounts of attempts up to the mid eighteenth century; indeed the only flying females were either classical deities and mythical creatures or witches. For women, any attempt at flight in the torrid heyday of their persecution in the sixteenth and seventeenth centuries would have entailed a double risk, of death in the undertaking or of execution as a witch.

After the intense attention given to matters of flight in the seventeenth century there was a shift away from prosthetic wings towards aircraft, or, in the words of historian Charles Gibbs-Smith, from 'flappers' to 'floaters'.[10] Lana de Terzi had pioneered the idea of using huge sealed globes to lift a small boat, and Tito Livio Burattini had produced the Flying Dragon for the Polish king Władysław IV. By 1709 another Catholic cleric, Bartolomeu de Gusmaõ, had persuaded the king of Portugal to back his invention of the Passarola ('swallow') – a pleasingly baroque and utterly implausible creation, images of which made the rounds of the European presses for decades to come. All over the continent inventors worked on flying chariot designs, among them Emanuel Swedenborg and the future balloonist Jean-Pierre Blanchard. The Cherub Chariot, the Vaisseau Volant and the Daedalian were, despite their evocative nomenclature, little different from the fictional apparatuses being devised by romantic novelists in the same period.

Tower jumpers continued, including the Marquis de Bacqueville who ended his much heralded flight across the Seine with two broken legs in a laundry woman's barge in 1742. The invention and refinement of the balloon would absorb the attention and excitement of almost everyone with aerial interests in the late eighteenth century, but some inventors continued to work on wingsuits and ornithopters. The Austrian clock-maker Jakob Degen used a hydrogen balloon to achieve enough lift for his 12-metre wings to function. He was set upon and injured by his spectators while preparing for a Paris flight in 1812. Presumably the aggression was triggered by a sense of false advertisement: Degen's ability to fly with wings had been the promised attraction, whereas he had used an everyday balloon as the means of ascent. This sorry incident indicates how, one form of reliable ascension having been achieved, spectators of flight nurtured much higher expectations of their winged men.

2   Windbags

> Ten times ten thousand hearts go palpitating; all
> tongues are mute with wonder and fear; till a shout,
> like the voice of seas, rolls after him on his wild
> way. He soars, he dwindles upwards; has become a
> mere gleaming circlet … like a new daylight Moon!
> Finally he descends, welcomed by the universe.
> – Thomas Carlyle, *The French Revolution* (1837)[11]

Crowds of spectators were a fundamental accessory to the first dependable method of flight, the balloon. The first launch of a 30-foot paper bag filled with hot air from burning straw was an advertisement for a family paper

mill near Lyons. The Montgolfier brothers waited until a large crowd had amassed before releasing their device. This ascent at Annonay in June 1783 was the first balloon flight in the Westen world, as well as a very effective publicity stunt. Not only were the brothers assured of fame for their invention, but they also unwittingly precipitated a surge in demand for a different paper product: prints and engravings of the new phenomenon of aerostation. Thomas Carlyle, in his 1837 book *The French Revolution*, included this in what he called 'The Paper Age', in which banknotes and books were printed as never before: 'Beautiful invention; mounting heavenward, so beautifully – so unguidably! … So, riding on windbags, will men scale the Empyrean.'[12]

As the Montgolfier brothers prepared to repeat their feat for King Louis XVI at Versailles, Dr Jacques Alexandre César Charles was experimenting with a second method of lifting a ballon. The English scientist Henry Cavendish had made the discovery of 'inflammable air' in the 1860s; it was then refined, and named hydrogen, by the French chemist Antoine Lavoisier.

Its utility as a rising agent had been tested by filling soap bubbles, but Charles devised a treated silk envelope and, no doubt inspired and informed by the Annonay success, organized the launch of a 30-foot gas balloon in front of a spectating public in late August 1783 at the Champs de Mars, now the site of the Eiffel Tower.

Upon its descent in the village of Gonesse, the balloon so startled villagers that they attacked it with pitchforks and muskets. Believing it to be a demonic eminence, they called a priest to bless the crumpled shell with holy water. (French countrymen were not alone in this quite reasonable alarm: the inhabitants of the small British town of Leominster were similarly unnerved when a small gas balloon, launched in London, alighted there later in 1783.) The French government issued a proclamation of reassurance: 'Anyone who should see such a globe, resembling the moon in an eclipse, should be aware that, far from being an alarming phenomenon, it is only a machine made of taffetas or light canvas, covered with a paper, that cannot cause any harm, and which will some day prove serviceable to the wants of society.'[13] Transport, survey and warfare all lay some distance in the future. For now, what society wanted was more balloon launches.

At 70 feet tall, the Montgolfière demonstrated a fortnight later at Versailles would have dwarfed the Charlière. It was painted in glorious colours with classical references and loaded with a symbolic live cargo of a sheep, a duck and a cockerel to test the possibility of survival in the upper atmosphere. At last the intricately designed gardens of Versailles might be viewed as they had been designed to be seen, if only at this point by livestock. Two months later the Montgolfiers were ready to send the first men into the air, the enthusiastic and dashing Jean-François Pilâtre de Rozier and François Laurent, Marquis d'Arlandes. The balloon rose from a hill overlooking the Champs de Mars, with the two pilots busily stoking their fire from either side of the gallery, and achieved a 27-minute flight over Paris. Upon landing, the bright green coat worn for show by Pilâtre was seized by a euphoric crowd and ripped apart for souvenirs.

Once again Charles was on the tail of the brothers and, only ten days after this first human ascent, the doctor himself and a companion, Nicolas-Louis Robert, went up in his gas balloon from the Tuileries Gardens in Paris. By now ballooning was the talk of the city and as many as 400,000 people, or half the city's population, came to watch. This was the biggest pre-revolutionary crowd the capital had ever attracted, and it is certainly possible to see how the dynamics of balloon ascents might have primed

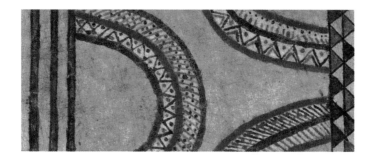

Machine Aérostatique de 126 p. de haut sur 100 p. de large.

Elevée dans les Champs appellés les Brotteaux, hors de la Ville de Lion, le 19 Janvier 1784, par M. Montgolfier, en vertu d'une Souscription de 12 p. par personne. Le 16 Janvier, ne provoquant pas l'effet de l'humidité que le balon avoit essuyé par les mauvais tems, on mit le feu, alors l'humide, raréfié et réduit en vapeurs corroda les toiles et mit le feu à la calotte, il fut détruit en une minute. L'ecole du 10 fit prendre des mesures plus réfléchies. Le 19 on fit secher les toiles, et on mit 2 heures à gonfler le balon, on l'on n'avoit employé çi devant que 27 minutes. Dans l'Etat de perfection on l'on crut qu'il était: M. Montgolfier, M. Pilâtre de Rozier, M. le Prince Charles de Ligne, M. le C de la Porte, M. le C de Dampierre, M. le C de Laurencin, et M. Fontaine de Lion, entrerent dans la galerie. On - Titans parut avec le fort élévée, ce fardeau immense s'éleva à la hauteur de 3000 pieds en 18 minutes a la satisfaction de plus de 100,000 spectateurs qui exprimoient leur enthousiasme par mille cris de joye. En forçant le feu pour s'élever plus rapidement il se fit une ouverture verticale, de 4 pieds, ce qui fut le terme du Voyage, qui ne dura que 15 minutes, et les Voyageurs descendirent dans une prairie près de Lion, sans aucun accident.

TOP: A swatch from the Montgolfière which ascended near Lyons in January 1784. BOTTOM: The same Montgolfière. It took up seven men, watched by 10,000 people. PAGE 32: The ascent of Charles and Robert from the Tuileries Gardens in December 1783 which attracted half the population of Paris as spectators. PAGE 33: In this British caricature a Montgolfier brother exclaims: 'Dis le de grande invention – Dis will immortalize my King, my Country, and myself. We will declare de War against our enemies: we will make des English quake, by gar.'

36

TOP: The return of M. Charles and M. Robert's balloon, 1 December, 1783.
BOTTOM: Consternation at Gonesse after the descent of the first unmanned gas
balloon, 27 August 1783. OPPOSITE: Launch at Versailles of the Montgolfière –
named Le Réveillon in honour of its decorator, Jean-Baptiste Réveillon, a wallpaper
designer – carrying a sheep, a duck and a cockerel, 19 September 1783.

the Parisian public for a different kind of mob sentiment less than a decade later. The flight lasted two hours, though Charles passed a further thirty-five minutes flying alone after the balloon rapidly relaunched when his companion stepped out of the gondola. He wrote an account of this remarkable experience, describing the 'sort of physical rapture' that being airborne produced in him: 'Such utter calm. Such immensity! Such an astonishing view.'[14] It constituted the first of a great deal of aerial travel writing.

Although the Montgolfiers had achieved the firsts, Charles's gas-filled silk proved the more reliable type of balloon. Used initially with hydrogen, followed by coal gas in the nineteenth century and helium in the twentieth, this design would continue to be the norm until propane burners made hot air balloons a viable alternative in the 1960s.

The print culture of this period was able to cater fast and in bulk to the growing public interest in aeronautics. There are dozens of versions of scenes of these initial ascents in existence, engraved for journals, broadsheets and souvenir handbills. Though the balloons themselves were of significant interest, it is also fascinating to see how they are framed in the engravings, almost always in portrait format to allow the balloon sufficient height in the picture space, with a crowd of onlookers, a central launching point and scenic detail in the background denoting one or other of the symbolic open spaces – the Tuileries, the Champs de Mars or Versailles. Occasionally collections of aeronautical prints show different states of an

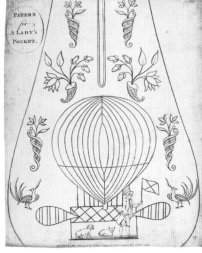

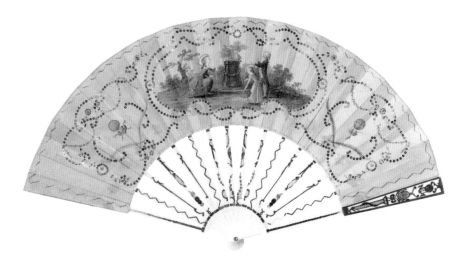

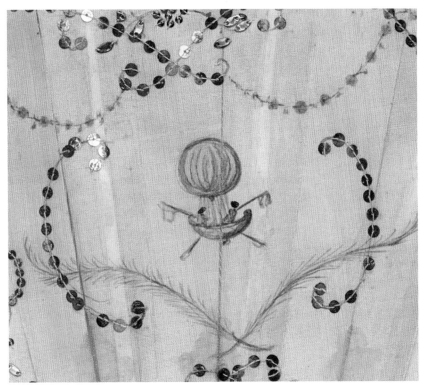

ABOVE: Fan with balloon imagery. OPPOSITE: 'Best Air Balloon' tobacco advertisement and design for a lady's pocket.

engraver's plate, where the setting and onlookers stay the same but the type of balloon is updated. Ballooniana was not restricted to print items. Handkerchiefs, snuff-boxes, earrings, tableware, fans and even pianos were decorated with aeronautical motifs.

40

In France the Académie des Sciences and the royal court supported the development of aeronautics, with the academy exerting control over who could fly and when. In Britain, where the president of the Royal Society, Joseph Banks, regarded the new invention with suspicion for its frivolity and apparent lack of utility, ballooning was an unregulated and privately financed enterprise. As balloonomania crossed the Channel in the summer of 1784, individuals all over the country began to experiment with small, unmanned gas and fire balloons. It was an Italian, Vincent Lunardi, who undertook the first manned flight. In raising the considerable capital needed to make and inflate a gas balloon, Lunardi employed charm and showmanship. He hired London's Lyceum Theatre and exhibited his new balloon to paying visitors. When inflated within the closed space, the balloon looked impressively enormous. Lunardi claimed that 20,000 people came to see it there. The balloon's residence at the theatre also worked as an effective

ABOVE: Vincent Lunardi at a launch from London's Tottenham Court Road (left)
and airborne after his ascent from Moorfields, September 1784 (right).
OPPOSITE: Jean-Pierre Blanchard and Dr Jeffries departing from Dover on the first
balloon crossing of the Channel, 7 January 1785.

advertisement for his launch, in September 1785, from the Artillery Grounds at Moorfields, which drew up to 150,000 spectators. As with many subsequent launches there was a delay of a few hours, during which the mood of the crowd grew restive and riotous, but Lunardi finally ascended to rapturous response and flew for several hours. On his descent he sold his story, with an exclusive interview, to the *Morning Post*, and once more exhibited the balloon, this time in the Pantheon.

Lunardi set the tone for ballooning in Britain, where it was a more festive and commercial affair than in France. One aeronaut, Jean-Pierre Blanchard, even came to England in the hope of finding finance when he was shut out of official French ballooning for his unscientific attitudes. He would go on to achieve the first Channel crossing with an American sponsor, Dr John Jeffries.

As with pre-ballooning flight attempts, the witnessing of an ascent was important to its success. Early balloonists never quite knew where they were going to descend; their landings usually summoned a crowd and they were always sure to approach a local landowner or official to sign an affidavit or *procès-verbal* to vouch for the duration of the flight. They gave much thought to appearances, not only in the decoration of their balloons and gondolas but also in their outfits and in the design of tickets and certificates. They were concerned to put on the greatest possible spectacle in the

ABOVE: Ticket to a Lunardi ascent.

air too; steering paddles, streamers and bells served to signal to the crowds below who, by subscription or by entry fee, had financed the ascent. As one aeronaut put it, the ascents were made possible by 'a tax on the curiosity of the public'; there was an acute awareness that the performance had to go on for as long as possible.[15] Onlookers did not always respond as expected, as the Marquis d'Arlandes noted after his ascent with Pilâtre de Rozier in 1783:

> I was astonished by the smallness of the noise our motion occasioned by our departure among the spectators; I thought they might be astonished and frightened, and might stand in need of encouragement, so I waved my arm with little success. I then drew out and shook my handkerchief, and immediately perceived a great movement in the yard.[16]

While they were dependent on crowds, balloonists were also at their mercy. No balloonist was ever killed by onlookers, but there are various examples of frustrated spectators storming the stage and destroying equipment. At a failing launch in Birmingham in December 1784, some of the 60,000 spectators who had travelled to witness the ascent began their own aerial bombardment, 'throwing sticks, stones, dead dogs and cats &c.' into the enclosure containing the balloon and the expensive front row seats. 'Peace' officers arrived, one person died in the scuffle and the Riot Act was read finally to disperse the crowd.

Mortality, an ever-present outcome for flight pioneers before ballooning, did not take long to associate itself with aeronautics. In 1785 Pilâtre de Rozier and his companion died attempting the first crossing of the Channel from France to England in a double balloon composed of a Montgolfière topped by a Charlière when this caught fire over Boulogne. In 1786 a local spectator in Newcastle upon Tyne was caught up in one of Lunardi's guy ropes and fell to his death. Commentators such as Benjamin Franklin and Horace Walpole soon conflated the informal rivalry between France and England in aeronautical matters with more serious political concerns and predicted aerial warfare, a scenario which played out vigorously in the cultural imagination. The French commander Napoleon's attempts to use balloons in military assaults in Austria and Egypt over the decade were largely failures, but an expression of some of the aggression felt towards the English in the late 1790s can be seen in the aerial bombardment of a building resembling an English warship on the Champ de Mars during the 1798 Festival of the Federation in Paris. Napoleon maintained a fondness for balloons; once he became emperor in 1804 he employed an official aeronaut to orchestrate patriotic aerial displays on fete days.

Balloons were deployed to display national and royal strength, and there were also projects to use them for international research. The research vessel Minerva, whose design by Étienne-Gaspard Robert (better known by his stage name, Professor Robertson) was circulated to the learned academies of Europe in 1804, had a 150-foot diameter and carried a boat large enough to house sixty passengers for a six-month trip around the globe. Despite being an academic vessel, the Minerva was bedecked with decorative emblems evoking and suggesting flight. Topped by a cockerel, the balloon featured small feathered wing tufts, several satellites and sails, and a rigid belt around its widest point, upon which observers could camp.

While inventors put their minds to making balloons navigable and detractors scoffed at their lack of useful application, ascents and displays continued to be a popular and profitable enterprise. An engraving of the Oxford-based balloonist James Sadler launching a balloon in Hackney in

Rupture du ballon du major Money, et sa chute dans la grande mer d'Allemagne, où il faillit périr le 18 juillet 1785.

Incendie du ballon et mort de Madame Blanchard, partie de Tivoli, et précipitée sur le toit de la maison n° 16, rue de Provence, le 6 juillet 1819.

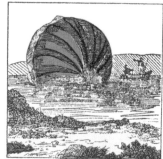

Godard, entièrement submergé et embarrassé dans les cordes de sa nacelle, est sauvé près de Grenelle par des pêcheurs, en juillet 1848.

Ascension équestre du lieutenant Gale, à Bordeaux ; descendu à Coulus, où l'aérostat, delesté du poids du cheval, enlève de nouveau l'aéronaute, trouvé le lendemain, 14 septembre 1850, horriblement mutilé.

Le jeudi 15 avril 1875, le Zénith partit de Paris vers midi ; il était monté par trois intrépides aéronautes : MM. Crocé-Spinelli, Sivel et Tissandier. — Ces savants, après avoir dépassé en une heure l'altitude de 8000 mètres, tombèrent dans un état d'anéantissement complet dû à la raréfaction de l'air. M. Crocé, s'étant réveillé un moment, jeta l'aspirateur qui tint dans la nacelle, et s'évanouit de nouveau. Le ballon remonta alors avec une vitesse vertigineuse à une altitude inconnue. A trois heures, M. Tissandier, reprenant ses sens à 6000 mètres, vit ses deux compagnons couchés dans la nacelle, la figure entièrement noire et la bouche pleine de sang.

CATASTROPHE DU ZÉNITH.

Ascension et mort d'Olivari à Orléans (Loiret), le 25 novembre 1802.

Il put cependant opérer la descente du ballon qui vint se déchirer contre des arbres, près de Ciron (Indre). Ce fut seulement après les avoir vainement appelés et secoués qu'il s'aperçut qu'ils étaient complètement asphyxiés. Les deux cadavres furent ramenés le 18 avril à Paris par M. Gaston Tissandier. Les obsèques eurent lieu le 20 au milieu du concours empressé et recueilli d'une affluence considérable ; l'Académie des sciences et tous les corps savants s'y étaient fait représenter officiellement et accompagnèrent jusqu'au Père Lachaise les deux malheureuses victimes de leur dévouement à la science.

Ascension de Robert et du duc de Chartres (Philippe-Égalité) à Saint-Cloud, suivie d'une descente périlleuse, le 15 juillet 1784.

Ascension de Sadler, à Bristol, à Dublin, à la suite desquelles il faillit périr dans la mer d'Irlande, en 1840.

Harris, parti de Londres le 29 septembre 1824, perd son gaz et descend avec une telle rapidité que l'aéronaute est tué sur le coup.

Imagerie de P. DIDION, à Metz.   Déposé

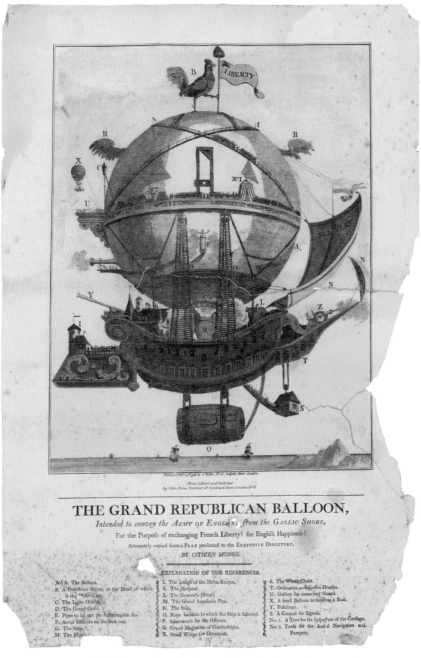

THE GRAND REPUBLICAN BALLOON,

Intended to convey the ARMY OF ENGLAND from the GALLIC SHORE,

For the Purpofe of exchanging French Liberty! for Englifh Happinefs!

Accurately copied from a PLAN prefented to the EXECUTIVE DIRECTORY,

BY CITIZEN MONGE.

EXPLANATION OF THE REFERENCES.

A A A. The Balloon.
B. A Pedeftrian Statue, in the Head of which is the Obfervatory.
C. The Light Houfe.
D. The Grand Gallic.
E. Pipes to let out the Inflammable Air.
F. Aerial Officers on the look out.
G. The Ship.
H. The Helm.

I. The Lodge of the Helm-Keeper.
K. The Hofpital.
L. The General's Houfe.
M. The Grand Aeroftatic Pipe.
N. The Sails.
O. Rope Ladders to which the Ship is faftened.
P. Apartments for the Officers.
Q. Grand Magazine of Combuftibles.
R. Small Wings for Ornament.

S. The Water Clofet.
T. Ordinaries and Coffee Houfes.
U. Gallery for mounting Guard.
X. A fmall Balloon to ferve as a Boat.
Y. Telefcope.
Z. A Cannon for Signals.
No. 1. A Tent for the Infpector of the Cordage.
No. 2. Tents for the Aerial Navigators and Pumpers.

ABOVE: The Minerva, here fitted out with a guillotine and repurposed by an English satirist as a vehicle of French asylum for British troops.
OPPOSITE: A French print showing a range of ballooning accidents.

ABOVE: Frontispiece and title page to an account of
two flights with André-Jacques Garnerin by British passengers, 1802.
OPPOSITE: James Sadler's ascent from Hackney, 1812.

1812 shows a micro-economy at work among the gathered spectators: buns
and prints are being hawked, while those who haven't paid for front row
seats clamber up trees and onto shoulders to observe the inflation.

If it wasn't an ascent it was a descent – the dropping of live cats, dogs
and sheep in parachutes was a frequent attraction. From 1797 balloons
also carried humans, even women. The French aeronauts André-Jacques
Garnerin and his niece Élisa both mounted elaborate shows based around
their ascent in a balloon which would then explode and leave them to
parachute back down, with fireworks thrown in for good measure. Sophie
Blanchard, widowed by her famous husband in 1808, went on to have a
spectacular career as a display balloonist. Sadly she perished after one of
her trademark aerial fireworks ignited the hydrogen of her vessel in 1819.
A handful of women had travelled in balloons since the time of their
invention, but these two were the first female career aeronauts.

There was a lull in the use of balloons for scientific investigations between
1830 and 1850, but that did not stop writers exploring the potential applica-
tions of aeronautics. Two influential American accounts were published in
the summer of 1835: Edgar Allan Poe's *The Unparalleled Adventure of One
Hans Pfaall*, in which a Rotterdam bellows maker escaped penury by flying

Ascension de Madam

Le Goût a

A Paris chez Martin

le 28 mars 1802.

Jour N.º 8.

Rue du Coq S.ᵗ Honoré.

MORT DE Mme BLANCHARD (1819)

to the moon in an insulated balloon gondola, and Richard Adams Locke's hoax article for the *New York Sun*, which claimed that the Enlightenment astronomer William Herschel had discovered inhabitants on the moon and described an expedition there by flying boat. Both accounts were echoed and imitated far and wide, with illustrations that differed little from the kind of blueprints circulated by inventors working in earnest on methods of aerial navigation. The balloon was also used as a didactic device by the American writer Peter Parley (Samuel Goodrich) in his *Balloon Travels* (1856), where the tutor Robert Merry and a band of children travel, unencumbered by the usual technicalities of ascent and descent, over Ireland, England and Continental Europe, learning their history and geography along the way.

Up to this point balloonists had taken one or at most two passengers along on their aerial voyages. In the first fifty years of aeronautics flight was available for vicarious enjoyment by spectators, consumers, and readers, and the individuals piloting the balloons had attained the status of heroic pioneers, in many cases justifiably. After the 1830s it became possible for more people at a time to experience flight. Ambitions were kindled for long-distance passenger travel. In 1834 the first London–Paris flights went on sale. The European Aeronautical Society announced that its 'rowing'

ABOVE: Frontispiece to *The Balloon Travels of Robert Merry*, 1856. OPPOSITE: Sophie
Blanchard at a performance for Napoleon in Milan, 1811 (left); the scene of her death
after her balloon caught fire in a fireworks show over Paris, 1819 (right).
PAGES 48–9: A plate from the French fashion magazine *Le Gout du Jour*, suggesting
suitable attire for a launch by Garnerin's wife Jeanne-Geneviève, March 1802.

balloon, the Eagle, would soon be in service from its London 'dockyard' in Kensington. The first Eagle had already exploded before its launch at the Champs de Mars, but Count Lennox, a French inventor of Scottish heritage, built its successor and exhibited it with confidence. The paddle-powered airship sat ground-bound for three months in Kensington and was then moved to Vauxhall Gardens for a fresh crowd, but the flights were never made. Soon the Eagle was forgotten, and was to be replaced in popular regard by the Royal Vauxhall Balloon.

Charles Green, the foremost British balloonist of the century, had begun his flying career aged around 40. He realized early on that he could replace hydrogen with cheaper coal gas, which in the 1820s was available via mains in London. Having made hundreds of ascents, he obtained a contract with the proprietors of Vauxhall Pleasure Gardens to launch a new enormous vessel in 1836. At 70,000 cubic feet, the Royal Vauxhall Balloon could carry eleven passengers in addition to Green. It was used both tethered – to lift a payload to 100 feet – and free, on several very well-attended ascents from the gardens in 1836.

ABOVE: Satire of Lennox's Eagle. OPPOSITE: 'The Century of Invention': a vision of the year 2000, printed on a linen handkerchief.

It was this balloon, with Green at the controls, that undertook the first long-distance air journey out of England. Carrying two passengers and an inordinate quantity of food and wine (estimated to sustain the party for three weeks), it set off from Vauxhall in November with no fixed destination but a distant one. Three days later the group landed in Nassau, Germany, and distributed their leftovers with largesse to the bystanders who helped them pack up the balloon. The journey was written up with great panache and verbosity by one of the party, Thomas Monck Mason. His account, *Aeronautica*, is a wonderful read. Large passages of it were lifted by Edgar Allan Poe for his fake news story about a balloon managing to cross the Atlantic several years later. Green did in fact propose to make the crossing using a balloon equipped with clockwork propellers, but he never found a sponsor.

The Royal Nassau, as it was rechristened, continued to ascend from Vauxhall and then from other central London sites such as Chelsea's Cremorne Gardens until Green's retirement in the early 1850s. Other passengers included the famous journalist Henry Mayhew, who wrote a memorable account of his ascent over the city whose lower aspects (both physical and moral) he already knew well. Aeronauts provided the public with diverse entertainments, angling for 'firsts' of every variety, from all-women ascents

54

UNDER THE DIRECT PATRONAGE OF HER MAJESTY,

ROYAL GARDENS, VAUXHALL.

GRAND DAY AND EVENING FETE,

NEXT TUESDAY, AUGUST 7, 1838.

ASCENT OF THE

Nassau Balloon

COMBINED WITH THE EVENING ENTERTAINMENTS.

The Ascent conducted by Mr. GREEN.

Places in the Car for Ten Persons.

Doors open at Half-past Four—Ascent at Half-past Five—Concert at Eight—Michael Boai,
Dramatic Piece, Living Statues, Dioramas, &c. follow, and the Fireworks at Half-past Ten.

Admission to the whole, ONE SHILLING AND SIXPENCE;
After the Ascent, to the whole of the Evening Amusements, ONE SHILLING!

PARTIES CAN DINE IN THE GARDENS.

☞ A Grand Naval Fete on Wednesday, 8th August.

[Balne, Printer, 38, Gracechurch Street.

ABOVE: Advertisement for a launch of Charles Green's
Nassau balloon at Vauxhall, with added entertainments, 1838.
OPPOSITE: Advertisement for a night flight by Mrs Graham, 1850.

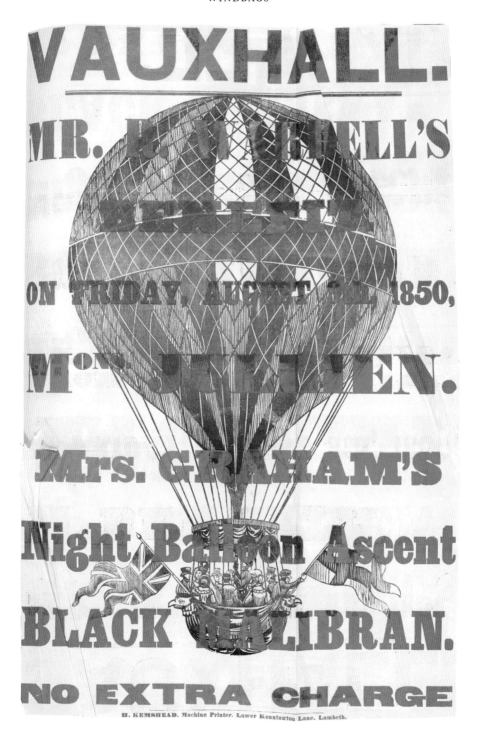

VAUXHALL.

MR. E. WARDELL'S

BENEFIT

ON FRIDAY, AUGUST 9th 1850,

Mons. JULLIEN.

Mrs. GRAHAM'S

Night Balloon Ascent

BLACK MALIBRAN.

NO EXTRA CHARGE

H. KEMSHEAD, Machine Printer, Lower Kennington Lane, Lambeth.

ABOVE: The descent of the Royal Vauxhall balloon in the Valley of Elbern,
Nassau, as reproduced in Thomas Monck Mason's account *Aeronautica*, 1838.
OPPOSITE: The same balloon over the Medway in Kent, at the beginning
of its journey east across Europe, 1836.

and night ascents to aerial menageries. Mrs Margaret Graham, a tenacious
and somewhat accident-prone balloonist, drew spectators in particularly
large numbers for that reason – seldom did her ascents take place unim-
peded by a spine-tingling snag. Moreover the very dynamic of the crowd
was often enough to provoke eruptions of dangerous unrest; balloons were
still being torn to shreds in rage when aeronauts did not perform as expected.

In the United States the balloonist John Wise undertook a voyage of
over 1,000 miles from St Louis, Illinois to Henderson, New York in 1859.
His next project was an Atlantic crossing, but like Green he failed to raise
the finance. Balloons had proved their staying power: though unreliable,
they were capable of carrying men over great distances. It took very close
attention to winds and currents to exert any influence over the direction
of flight, but the seeds had been sown for a new kind of air travel, even if
only in fantasy.

Afloat

> To be alone in a balloon at a height of fourteen or
> fifteen thousand feet [...] is like nothing else in
> human experience. It is one of the supreme things
> possible to man. No flying machine can ever better
> it. It is to pass extraordinarily out of human things.
> – H. G. Wells, *The War in the Air* (1908)[17]

By the 1860s the possibilities of free ballooning had been thoroughly explored. Hope in the potential of balloons to offer useful services, such as transport, survey, and exploration, was dwindling. Their entertainment value was well established but, without the attraction of novelty, aeronautical entertainers were hard pressed to find new draws for audiences. This chapter covers the period in the second half of the nineteenth century when windbags flourished, expanding into colossal crowd lifters and stretching into lozenge-shaped airships. Buoyancy had been achieved; dirigibility was the next goal. Chapter 4 addresses parallel developments in those experimenting with heavier-than-air aviation. In fact, both schools achieved success around the turn of the twentieth century.

The emblematic balloon of this period was Le Géant (The Giant). Built in 1863 by the consummate publicist Félix Nadar, this enormous gas balloon, with its two-storey wicker cabin, was conceived to test the limits of lighter-than-air aviation. At 210,000 cubic feet, it was three times larger than Green's Royal Nassau. Nadar, an eccentric but well-connected Parisian photographer, was already an aeronaut, having conducted experiments in aerial photography through the 1850s that resulted in the first patent in this area. He was convinced that the future lay with heavier-than-air aviation, but decided to work first with a tried and tested formula in order to raise funds to invest in further research. Several other aerial entrepreneurs had set out to build giant balloons, for scientific missions into the atmosphere or, tethered, to carry large numbers of paying passengers into the air. Nadar's plan was to create a balloon that could travel far around the globe, achieve fame and notoriety, and put air travel in the news. He was familiar enough with the workings of the mid-nineteenth-century press to realize that any outcome, however hair-raising, would give him publicity. He was friends with most of the literary figures in Paris, having taken their portraits in his studio, and the emerging novelist Jules Verne acted as the secretary of his aerial society. The society published a journal, *L'Aéronaute*, filled with prolific notes and illustrations on the construction and progress of Le Géant.

After a successful maiden voyage, carrying a handful of very rich passengers some distance from the Champs de Mars, Le Géant was launched on a long-distance voyage eastwards. This was not such a success: though it carried its crew of six (including Nadar and his wife) for seventeen hours, it had a terrible and protracted landing in Germany, in which everybody was badly injured. Nadar convalesced in the glow of avid press attention, giving endless iterations of accounts of the journey, then sued his pilot to generate more news. Shortly afterwards he produced a manifesto, the *Right to Fly*, in which he argued that the future of flight lay in aerial locomotives rather than in balloons.

This partnering of what was perceived to be an obsolete technology, that of gas balloons, with a quest for the next step in a different technology, of gliders and motors, seems strange now. But it was a pairing that was both logical and inspiring. Despite rare successes (which will be reviewed in Chapter 4), fixed wing development was slow over the nineteenth century, but it was becoming increasingly clear that glider flight would be achieved at some point. In the meantime there was renewed scientific interest in meteorology, and a balloon was the only option for aerial fieldwork. The first national aeronautical association in the world, founded in 1852, was the Société Aérostatique et Météorologique de France, which indicated that ballooning and weather science were regarded with the same seriousness. When the British Association for the Advancement of Science decided to fund meteorological investigations in the upper atmosphere, it commissioned a balloon, the biggest yet in Britain. Henry Coxwell, the balloonist who took over from Green as the most respectable British sky pilot, had a 93,000-foot balloon made: the Mammoth took its maiden flight in the summer of 1862. It could hold eleven passengers, but regularly carried just Coxwell and a nominated meteorologist, James Glaisher. On its third fact-finding ascent, from Wolverhampton on 5 September, it rose to 30,000 feet – a height at which Coxwell and Glaisher found, to their

ABOVE: The etching of James Glaisher 'insensible at 30,000 feet' produced
shortly after his flight with Henry Coxwell in September 1862 and reproduced
in his *Travels in the Air*, 1870. PAGE 58: Title page of *Nadar's
A Terre et en l'Air… Memoires du Géant*, 1864.

cost, that it was barely possible to breathe. Glaisher passed out and Coxwell
found that his hands were too numb to pull the valve line, but managed
to do so with his teeth. Both descended to tell the tale, which then circled
the world in newspapers and magazines, complete with engravings of the
dramatic moment. To Glaisher's chagrin, it was the peril rather than the
weather science that caught the headlines.

Glaisher was instrumental in the foundation of the Aeronautical Society of Great Britain in 1866; he inaugurated its first meeting with a rejection
of the showmanship and spectacle that, to him, dogged the development of
useful ballooning. But he could not shake off the public appetite for aerial
exploits and sublime scenes, and in 1870 published his ballooning stories in
a compilation together with those by the French aeronauts Camille Flam-
marion, Wilfrid de Fonvielle and Gaston Tissandier: *Travels in the Air*.
Albert Tissandier, Gaston's brother and an architect and artist, frequently
ascended with him to sketch meteorological phenomena; his arresting
etchings illustrated the book, which soon went into a second edition.

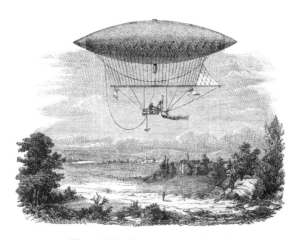

ABOVE: Henri Giffard's steam-powered airship, 1852.
OPPOSITE: Giffard's Colossus, a steam-winched, tethered balloon
with a capacity for 50 passengers, at the Paris Exhibition, 1878.

There was not a one-way technological progression from ballooning
to powered flight. Many inventors experimented with both. The French
engineer Henri Giffard designed the first steam-powered airship, flying
seventeen miles in 1852 (in very calm weather), but then used his research
into steam engines to build powered winches to raise and lower the tether
of enormous captive balloons. Giffard's balloons were used by the scientific
community and also as public entertainment; indeed, both kinds of observer
intermingled in the basket of the Captive, which held twenty-nine passengers. It was installed outside the Crystal Palace in Sydenham to attract
visitors to the first Aeronautical Exhibition in 1868. Fliers were promised a
view of 'one-tenth of the whole of England' from the 1,000-foot zenith.[18]
Take-up seems to have been unimpressive, for by 1869 the proprietor of the
Captive was offering journalists a free lunch in the air to boost coverage of
the experience. Nevertheless, the tethered balloon experience did become
more popular. Giffard's Colossus, unveiled at the 1878 Paris Exhibition,
carried fifty passengers at once, enabling 35,000 people to ascend to 500 feet
in the summer season alone. Becoming airborne – experiencing ascension
and seeing the view from above – was beginning to be conceived as something that was in the public interest.

Ballooning was still a sport for crowds, but the element of spectacle now
lay not only in the appearance and ascent of the balloon but also in the views

64

and sensations it offered its passengers. Tethered balloons were installed in pleasure gardens, including Vauxhall and Cremorne, and afforded a great many more people an aerial experience. Contrast the tens of thousands of passengers of one summer in 1870s Paris with the total number of people thought to have ascended in a balloon in the British Isles before 1836: 313.[19]

With their bulk and fabric, balloons were a prominent visual presence in the sky, even more so as their girth increased in the latter part of the nineteenth century. They had long been decorated with the names of patrons, with allusions to royal figures or in patriotic colours, and served as a floating advertisement for and a reminder of flight. Their symbolic potency gave balloons a weight well beyond their practical impact, in spite of the very minor part they played in great geopolitical events of the nineteenth century – in the American Civil War or the Siege of Paris. A patchwork envelope sewn from the silk gowns of Southern belles was a standard for Confederate defiance; a globe rising silently at dusk from within a beleaguered capital city to overfly the bayonets and rifles of Prussian troops was as much a symbol of Parisian resilience as a conduit for the 'airmail' and politicians it carried out.[20]

Balloons stood for hope in attaining a more practical means of flight. Veteran vessels were sent on tour as objects of interest even after their useful life was over. As the increasingly leaky Géant, which never fully recovered from its German ordeal, was trundled around Europe, so too were thousands of copies of Nadar's manifesto and a supporting, hyperbolic *Letter on Flight* by the famous émigré writer Victor Hugo. The fuss around Le Géant helped sales of the novel that Jules Verne had already written, *Five Weeks in a Balloon* (1863; English translation 1870), which imagined a plucky trio of British adventurers surveying Africa from above. The novel played to the popular European perception of the continent: the crowds that Verne's balloon encountered were hostile, displaying the savage and ignorant traits commonly attributed to rural Africans, which allowed for numerous thrilling escapes and episodes of technological one-upmanship by the European aeronauts. Verne's *Robur le Conquerant*, or *Clipper of the Clouds* (1886; English translation 1887), departed further into speculative fiction with the Albatross, a perpetually buoyant cardboard aircraft suspended from airscrews which secretly patrolled the skies equipped with bombs. Once more, the separation of civilization and rude natives is depicted with relish as the Albatross attacks a barbaric mass sacrifice ceremony in Dahomey.

The invention and refinement of a motor light enough to be carried into the air by gas balloon in the second half of the nineteenth century

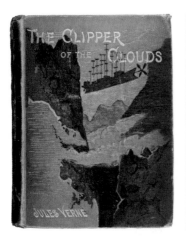

ABOVE: The Albatross to the rescue: cover and illustration from the English version of Jules Verne's *The Clipper of the Clouds*, 1887. OPPOSITE: The French balloon Tricolore on an ascent on 6 June 1874. It probably carried French aeronaut Jules Duruof and his wife; the following month they would attempt a flight from Calais in a bad wind and land in the North Sea.

ABOVE: Alberto Santos-Dumont lands at his front door at 9, rue
Washington in Paris in the late 1890s. OPPOSITE: Santos-Dumont
rounds the Eiffel Tower to win the Deutsch de la Meurthe prize, 1901.

changed the texture of aeronautical ambition. In 1860 Étienne Lenoir's gas
engine encouraged inventors to turn their minds to aircraft and led to the
formation of aeronautical societies; in 1876 the German engineer Nikolaus
Otto developed the petrol engine, which was modified by Gottlieb Daimler a decade later to power automobiles. *Fin de siècle* aviation had much in
common with the new culture of motoring, with aero clubs quickly being
formed to follow auto clubs; the wealthy and intrepid often joined both.
The most spectacular achievement of the period was the Brazilian Alberto
Santos-Dumont's rounding of the Eiffel Tower in 1901 in his sixth dirigible
balloon. A rich and dapper aeronaut, Santos-Dumont was already famous
for his idiosyncratic cigar-shaped balloons, and this was his third attempt
to win a large cash prize set up by another French aero club member. His
previous dramatic failures had won him the sympathy and attention of
much of Paris, and he was frequently accosted with kisses on the city streets.

Santos-Dumont was hailed internationally at the time as the first man
to achieve powered flight, but the lack of rigidity in his aircraft left them
vulnerable to jack-knifing in high winds or with the loss of gas. From the
1880s onwards European inventors had been taking advantage of cheaper
aluminium to experiment with making rigid frames for the elongated
balloons that were now understood to have the best dirigible properties.
In Germany Count Zeppelin built his first airship with an aluminium
frame and Daimler engines in 1900; though this model was not successful,

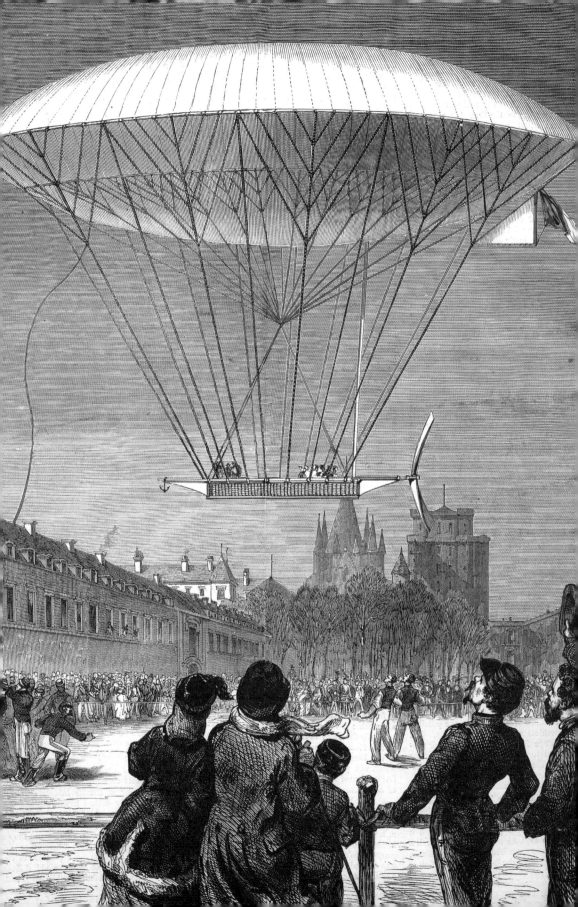

ABOVE: Count Zeppelin, as portrayed on the front cover of *Jugend* magazine, 1908. OPPOSITE: The Navigating Balloon of M. Dupuy de Lôme makes the front page of the *Graphic*, 24 February 1872.

Zeppelin went on to produce the most effective airships in Europe. In England the son of a family of balloon pilots, Stanley Spencer, funded his experimental powered balloon, which was not rigid but had a bamboo gondola with a small motor, by pre-selling twenty-five flights to a baby food company in Peckham to advertise their product. After several trials Spencer succeeded in a flight over London in 1902 which drew great attention from the crowds below. Despite setbacks in the dirigibility of his aircraft, he was able to make a livelihood from constructing balloons and selling advertising to other companies; in 1909 one of his powered balloons, emblazoned with the slogan 'Votes for Women', flew an Australian suffragette, Muriel Matters, over the capital for a leaflet drop.

The Wright brothers' achievement of aeroplane flight in 1903, along with the progress made by many Europeans with gliders and engines in the next decade, did not halt airship development. The buoyancy and aerial longevity of the latter were seen as far more promising for passenger or freight services. In 1910 the German government, which had not been interested in Count Zeppelin's early airship experiments, endorsed his work and encouraged him to set up a passenger service. By 1914 the Deutsche

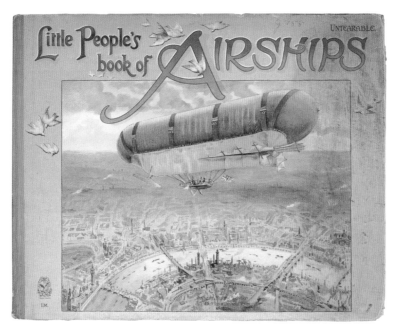

TOP: Passengers travelling in the Zeppelin LZ 3, 1907. BOTTOM: British dirigible
Nulli Secundus illustrated on the cover of a children's book of airships, 1912.
OPPOSITE: The first passenger service in a Zeppelin, from Friedrichshafen
to Dusseldorf, Germany, as announced in the *Sphere*, 2 July 1910.

LEFT: Poster for J.M. Gaites's musical comedy 'The Air Ship', *c.*1898.
RIGHT: Dolly Shepherd's aerial rescue of Louie May, as depicted in
the *Illustrated Police Budget*, 1908.

Luftfahrt Actien Gesselschaft had carried over 17,000 passengers around
Germany. The British government, which at last decided to fund aeronautics by establishing an Army Balloon School in 1888, began work on airships
in 1902; in 1907 the 'Army Dirigible Number One', Nulli Secundus, made
several test flights. After it was damaged in high winds, it was modified into
NS II, or, rather ridiculously, Nulli Secundus 'the Second'. It made a flight
at Farnborough in July 1908 that was watched by thousands of people. The
airship was scrapped soon afterwards and its motor used to power 'Army
Aeroplane Number One'.

Both these pioneer aircraft were first flown by the same man, 'Colonel'
Samuel Franklin Cody. Cody's involvement in official aviation shows clearly
the government's lack of strategy in research and development, and how
aviation was still closely linked with entertainment. Cody was an American
music hall entertainer who had toured several successful horse-riding stunt
shows around Great Britain and who spent his spare time flying box kites
with his sons; he used the box office takings from his shows on aircraft
experiments. The most famous female aeronaut of this period was also
an entertainer. Dolly Shepherd combined a day job in her aunt's ostrich
feather emporium with a daring career as a parachute artiste. She achieved

TOP: The start of the 1908 Gordon Bennett Balloon race at the Schmargendorf gasworks, Berlin. BOTTOM LEFT: Flight was a recurring motif in the French novelist Albert Robida's imagining of the century to come, *Le Vingtième Siècle: La Vie Eléctrique*, 1892. BOTTOM RIGHT: Cover of *The Polyphemes* by F. Hernaman-Johnson (1906), which imagines man's response to an invasion by giant ants in flying machines.

ABOVE: Illustration by A. C. Michael of the London-Brighton road passing through
Bun Hill, home of H. G. Wells's protagonist Burt Smallways in *The War in the
Air*, 1907. PAGE 74: Illustration by Frank X. Leyendecke and H. Reuterdahl from
Rudyard Kipling's 'With the Night Mail', 1909. PREVIOUS PAGE: Scene from Albert
Robida's *Le Vingtième Siècle: La Vie Eléctrique*, 1892.

widespread admiration for carrying out the first air to air rescue of a fellow performer in 1908.

As in the early years of ballooning, scenes of aggression were played out in festive and cultural arenas. The cinema distributor Charles Urban made *The Airship Destroyer* in 1909, in which a fleet of bomber airships was destroyed by a young man's flying machine. After the impressive flight over London of the army's Beta airship in 1910, the Coliseum theatre installed a 20-foot-long model dirigible that could glide out of the proscenium and over the audience, dropping paper toys instead of bombs. Drury Lane Theatre put on *The Spy Thriller* in 1913, which featured the shooting down of a foreign airship by a British gunboat. Of course, the potential to convert the vessels to military use underpinned government investment, and during the First World War numerous bombing raids over England *were* carried out by Zeppelins. The British airship R34 was developed for retaliation, but at the war's end it was sent in the opposite direction, to America, achieving the first Atlantic crossing by airship only months after two British pilots had flown the first aeroplane non-stop across the ocean.

By the second decade of the twentieth century ballooning was at last eclipsed. It continued as a privileged leisure activity, with a continuing appeal to those who were less interested in noisy motors. The Gordon Bennett Ballooning Cup, established in 1906, encouraged long-distance voyages. The emblematic globe had been replaced by an even more comical cucumber-shaped inflatable. Once more it was a gift to satirists; the phallic appearance of the airship furnished many a postcard and cigarette card with the potential for innuendo. But it was fully absorbed into the popular consciousness as an object of menace, as well as of mirth, provoking fears of attack with phantom airship viewings reported up and down the country in the 1910s. And, unlike the aeroplane, it was seen as the future of passenger aviation.

Established fiction writers of the day had no trouble envisaging the future of airships. Rudyard Kipling produced several serialized stories in which a huge network of sky routes, studded with colour-coded aerial beacons, hosted fleets of mail-carrying airships crewed by rugged sea-dogs. In 1907 H. G. Wells wrote *The War in the Air*, which bristled with airships as well as gyrocopters and balloons; it was published in the *Pall Mall Magazine*. Wells's prediction that powered flight would lead to aerial warfare was borne out by subsequent events. 'I told you so. You damned fools' was the epitaph he proposed for himself in the mid 1940s.

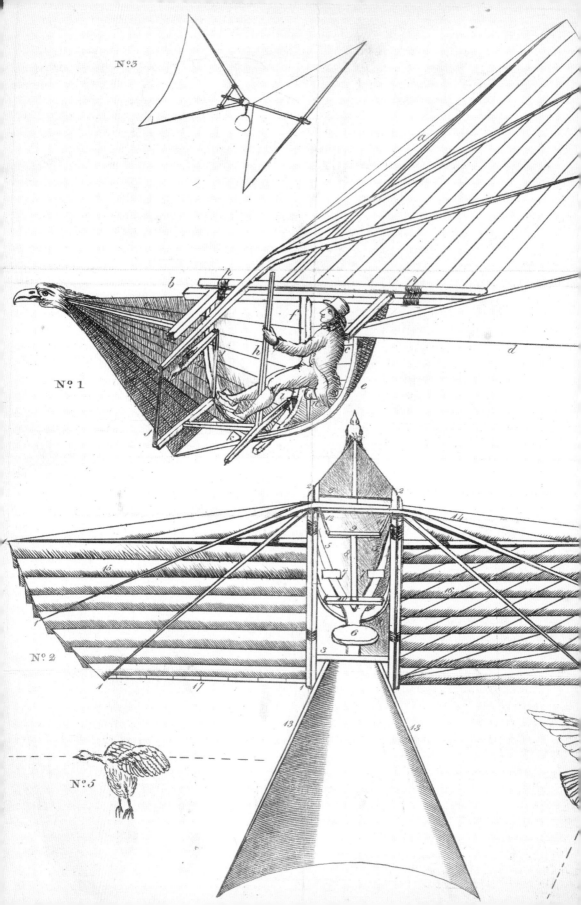

4 Wind Wrestlers

> I have not the smallest molecule of faith in aerial
> navigation other than ballooning.
> – Lord Kelvin (1896)[21]

All through the nineteenth century, men (again, no women) endeavoured to produce a more navigable aircraft than the balloon. They failed. While working airships were developed from the 1880s, these were unreliable. But this was the century that more productive work than ever was done in the service of flight. Numerous talented inventors studied, modelled and tested flight machines, forming an international milieu of aeronautical research that was on the cusp of success by 1900. Still, as late as 1896 it appeared to renowned physicist William Thomson, Lord Kelvin, that their efforts would lead to nothing.

The men who laboured on blueprints and trials were different from most of the aerial enthusiasts we have come across so far. They worked in private. They were either self-funded or had secured investment after taking out patents. They did not court spectacle. But they were certainly influenced by the phenomenon of flight as entertainment. The most remarkable British inventor, George Cayley, was transfixed by flight at the age of 10, when news of the successes of the Montgolfiers and Charles reached Yorkshire. He sketched potential flight machine parts in his schoolbooks and scratched an outline of a fixed-wing glider onto a silver disc in 1799. He was continuously experimenting with flight devices and aerodynamics and published his first papers on the subject in 1809, in a rush to get into print after he heard, incorrectly, that Jakob Degen had made a successful winged flight (see page 30).

That a coterie of dedicated inventors was now investigating aeronautics did not stop wider experimentation with flight. Cayley included instructions for a simple airscrew with corks and feathers in his 1809 paper, and it is not hard to see its appeal as a toy. Kites became very popular in Europe in the nineteenth century. The second half of the century saw an intense period of development of complex, weight-bearing kites, which aided inventors around the world in developing aeroplanes. But kites also had an important function as toys in lifting the sights of the young. Their appeal to Victorian children was made much of by literary moralists, who drew analogies between the kite and the wayward child. Flight was the worst possible ending for juvenile kite-fliers, who might be carried away after exhibiting excessive pride or a headstrong nature.

It was on the basis of Cayley's discoveries that the century's most famous heavier-than-air craft was designed. W. S. Henson's Aerial Steam Carriage, Arial [sic] for short, was advertised widely from April 1843. Ten years after the European Aeronautical Society offered a Channel crossing by airship, the Aerial Transit Company was set up to take bookings for flights. In fact the aircraft was only just being built in model form, and its full-sized prototype never flew. But, as a result of astute publicity by one of the company directors – who commissioned attractive views of Arial over international landscapes, which were published in the illustrated papers – it became a Victorian icon and was reproduced on plates and silk handkerchiefs. In fine aeronautical tradition it also furnished a fake news story: the

TOP & BOTTOM: Arial over the Thames and at a station in 'Hindoostan'
in publicity plates for Henson's Aerial Steam Carriage, 1843. OPPOSITE: Design for a
steam-powered airship from 'Practical remarks on aerial navigation' by Sir George
Cayley, 1837. PAGE 78: Design from 'A treatise upon the art of Flying
by mechanical means' by Thomas Walker, a portrait painter from Hull inspired
by bird flight, 1810.

Glasgow Constitutional announced that it had achieved flight over the River Clyde before exploding and dropping its pilot into the water, and *The Times* repeated the news in good faith.

Much the work on Arial had been done in spare sheds of lacemaking factories in Chard, Somerset, where its inventors were based. Henson did carry out some trials with models in London in the semi-public spaces of the Adelaide Gallery, off the Strand, and the Hippodrome at Bayswater, but the first successful flight of an engine-driven model in public was undertaken by his colleague John Stringfellow. After Henson despaired of aeronautics and emigrated to the United States, Stringfellow went on to experiment with kites and less complex model gliders, which, like Arial, were launched by sliding down a long wire. In 1848 he was offered a large tent at Cremorne Gardens to install the wire and glider for exhibition purposes. An American newspaper reported that it 'excited considerable attention and surprised all the spectators by its wonderful performance'.[22] Stringfellow also created a steam-powered triplane for the first Aeronautical Exhibition. This created a sensation among visitors by whizzing down a wire suspended in the nave of the Crystal Palace and won him the society's grand prize.

The Arial and its progeny caught the imagination in a way that only balloons had done to date. Broadside ballads expressed a curious mixture of ridicule and ambition about Henson's aircraft and the projected global passenger service. 'It matters not, I understand, whichever way the wind is / They'll waft you in a day or so, right bang into the Indies!' went one,[23] while another ran:

> The very skies are brightening up –
> The anxious clouds are clearing,
> To cheer brave Henson as he through
> The Milky Way is steering.
> The twinkling stars appear to think
> The sight will prove a treasure
> And the Comet seems delighted
> For he – wags his tail with pleasure!![24]

The Arial, referred to here as the Comet, had a striking fan-shaped tail. In a strange coincidence, the first jet-powered airliner in Britain would also be named the Comet.

Dr W. D. Miller's 'aerostat' ornithopter design, 1843.

Persuading others of airworthiness by suggestion, rather than by proof, was an effective strategy. Dr W. D. Miller's ornithopter design, featuring a well-proportioned and resolute male figure in garters suspended at some height over a picturesque landscape, was also widely circulated in 1843. The Aerial Man was shown taking to the air over Greenwich Park.

These images of nonchalant fliers contrasted sharply with the other genre of aerial picture that was often widely published, the disaster scene. An appetite had been established for dramatic falls by ballooning accidents; mid- and late nineteeth-century engineers also provided moments of high drama. Robert Cocking, a watercolour painter who had witnessed the first English descent of the great parachutist André-Jacques Garnerin (see page 47) in 1802, devoted his later life to working on better models. Having conducted tests with models launched from London's Monument, he persuaded Charles Green to take him to 5,000 feet in his balloon in 1837 in order to trial his new design. The structure of his parachute, an inverted cone, crumpled and Cocking fell to his death at Lee Green. Many images circulated afterwards, partly generated by fundraisers for Cocking's widow, which, ironically, consisted of more balloon ascents. In 1874 a Belgian inventor, Vincent de Groof, was taken up in his ornithopter by the balloonist Joseph Simmons from Cremorne Gardens. Upon its release from the balloon, the wings buckled and de Groof plummeted into a Chelsea street;

SCENE AT THE REAR

FIREMEN SAVING SOME OF THE ANIMALS FROM DEATH

RUSSIAN BEAR

HER & SISTER- MANCH.

PRIZE F

THAMES

SUICIDE OF

TERRIBLE BALLOON ACCIDENT

ABOVE: Robert Cocking's fatal descent at Lee, Kent, 24 July 1837.
OPPOSITE: The cover of *The Illustrated Police* News, 14 June 1884.

Otto Lilienthal in his Big Biplane, or double-decker glider,
photographed by Dr R. Neuhauss, 1895.

he died soon afterwards. In their posthumous portraits both Cocking and De Groof wear a look of glazed panic, which was no doubt relished by viewers shuddering at their foolhardiness.

Death continued to haunt flight attempts. In the 1890s two well-respected glider engineers, the German Otto Lilienthal and the British Percy Pilcher, were killed in test flights. It was not always the flight itself that proved fatal, but the high stakes. Alphonse Pénaud, a French inventor who produced the first stable models of helicopter and ornithopter that could be launched into flight with a rubber band, committed suicide after his ambitious 1876 design for a full-sized monoplane was ridiculed and failed to secure funding. In fact Pénaud's influence reached far further than many of his contemporaries'. His designs were made into popular toys and, as children, Wilbur and Orville Wright were given a Pénaud-type helicopter by their father.

The popular sense of the potential of powered flight was heady. Music hall songs often riffed on celestial themes. Even though balloon ascents to a few thousand feet were a relatively common phenomenon, in songs balloons transported travellers into space. One song published in 1896 looked forward, prophetically, to 1903 as a date when flight would be achieved:

From the earth we will soar, we'll be Kings of new fields
As we search the fair regions so old
We'll pass the bright stars, near all the large orbs
And see if the moon's made of gold
We'll fly o'er the deep, and lands unknown
Ne'er trod by man nor foe
We'll ride soft winds where storms are unheard
Though seen in the clouds far below.[25]

Experiments all over the world continued in the 1880s and 1890s, connected and facilitated by figures such as Octave Chanute and Samuel Pierpoint Langley, the secretary of the Smithsonian Institution. But, for all the sharing, there was also secrecy and rivalry. The Wright brothers, having started experimenting with flight in earnest upon the news of Lilienthal's death, took their first sustained leaps from the earth in 1903. But, once they were working with a mechanically refined aeroplane, which drew crowds of spectators in 1905, they ceased flying until they had secured their patents and a contract for fear of copycats.

News of the Wrights' success circulated in Europe, but was not widely believed. French, British and German inventors continued to work on their own flying machines. Finally, after some years spent offering their designs to several governments, with the help of a New York agent and, in Britain, the 73-year-old widow Lady Jane Taylor, the Wright brothers reconciled themselves to proving their superiority through demonstration.

Wilbur Wright sailed to Europe to undertake a series of very well-attended flights in the summer of 1908, the first of which was at Le Mans, in France. This description of a later Wright ascent at Pau, in the French Pyrenees, provides a flavour of the scene:

Are you ready?
Up to this there had been quite a loud hum of conversation from the people assembled, but now a hush fell on the assembly, a pause almost of dread.
Let's go!
The weights fell, and with whirling propellers the fairylike machine tore along the rail to the end by the turn of one lever, and at twelve minutes past four it soared into the air, turning and wheeling up and down

as graceful as an albatross, showing the perfect
command which the aviator had over every movement
and every part of the machine.[26]

Even though it still had to be launched along rails to get into the air, the Wright Flyer astonished onlookers. The control exhibited by Wilbur Wright surpassed that achieved by any other aspiring aviator. The enthusiasts took note, and the quality of aircraft improved markedly over the next year. Wright himself was adored by the French public, and Lord Northcliffe published a personal profile of the reticent American in the *Daily Mail*. The British government was still reluctant to commit itself, all the while conducting its own research secretly. Finally it was decided in May 1909 to let private enterprise undertake designs and not to buy Wright Flyers nor to sponsor them. A nascent industry began, with several aircraft firms, catalogues advertising aeroplane parts, an aerodrome run by the Royal Aero Club, and two magazines, *Flight* and the *Aero*, started in the spring.

The year 1909 was also the first of powered flight as spectacle. The first French air week, sponsored by champagne houses, took place in Rheims in August. The balloonist Gertrude Bacon went alone to the show, and begged a ride from pilot Roger Sommer, making her the first Englishwoman to fly in an aeroplane. Of the thirty-eight aircraft that took part, none were British, though the competition was won by the English-born pilot Henri Farman, followed by the Anglo-French pilot Hubert Latham. The crowds shouted the names of the pilots with unanimous enthusiasm as they flew in turn around pylons. The same summer an air show was put on at Brescia in Italy. It was attended by Franz Kafka who, along with his friends, was eager to see the French aviator Louis Blériot fly. Kafka describes the mixture of anxiety and wonder they felt when, after much delay, the pilot took to the air.

> Devotedly everyone looks up at him; there is no room in anybody's heart for anyone else. He flies a small circle and then appears almost directly above us. And everyone looks with outstretched neck as the monoplane falters, is controlled by Blériot, and even climbs. What is happening? Here above us, there is a man twenty meters above the earth, imprisoned in a wooden frame, and defending himself against an invisible danger which he has taken on of his own free will. But we are standing below, pushed away, without existence, and looking at this man.[27]

THE SPHERE

GEO. MORROW.

AVIATION NUMBER

PRICE SIXPENCE.

200.000F. de PRIX
GRAND
SEMAI
Montaut
D'AVIATION D
REIMS DU 22 AU 29 AOÛT 1909 CHAMPA

ABOVE: Pilots Hubert Latham (left) and Claude Grahame-White (right) compete
at a 1910 aviation meet. OPPOSITE: Aviators are ecstatically welcomed by this female
spectator in the poster for the Rheims Aviation Week, drawn by Ernest Monteaux.
PAGE 89: Competitors in the 1909 Rheims air week are watched by the figure of
Hermes. Aviation issue of *The Sphere*, artwork by George Morrow, 28 August 1909.

Earlier in his article, Kafka had remarked on how, as a mere standing
visitor, he felt invisible to the Italian aristocrats occupying the grand-
stand. But Blériot's feat rendered everyone – aristocrat or not – 'without
existence'. The pilot had, for Kafka, achieved the ultimate alienation by
distancing himself from the world's surface, defying its gravitational pull.
This only made him more enthralling to spectators. Crowds flocked to
the airfield in greater and greater numbers. A new railway was laid from
Rheims to the site of the air show in anticipation of a huge influx of foot
visitors, a significant proportion of the 500,000 who attended over the
week. The failure of rail companies to foresee an increase in traffic for the
Paris air show led to incensed crowds of stranded passengers tearing up
the station at Juvisy, as the Swiss architect Le Corbusier recalled. Better
infrastructure was necessary and, as the popularity of other spectator
sports such as football and motor racing increased, ways were found to
manage the flow and accommodation of unprecedently large audiences.
These would soon be put to different use in a context of mobilization and
military transport.

Initially the only way for pilots to make money from the new technology was to set up flying schools. The Wright brothers established a school

92

TOP: The Paris Air Show in the Grand Palais, October 1910. BOTTOM: The Wright Flyer on display at the Paris Air Show, 1910. OPPOSITE: The French Captain Lucas-Girardville on a Wright Flyer, from *The Sketch*, 1909.

at Pau, in France, as did Blériot. In Britain schools also tended to cluster in locations that offered favourable conditions for flying and landing. One such was Hendon, just north of London; another was Brooklands in Surrey, where a school was founded by Hilda Hewlett, the first British woman to obtain an air licence and the future proprietor of the Hewlett & Blondeau aircraft factory. Hewlett was exceptional in her career on the business side of aviation, which was otherwise dominated by men. Whereas many French women had flown both as passengers and as pilots by 1914, in Britain women were actually barred from several schools. The 'Flying Countess', Kathleen, Lady Drogheda, earned her sobriquet simply as a regular passenger.

In October 1911 the first British flying meetings were held at Blackpool and Doncaster. At Blackpool Hubert Latham flew his Antoinette aeroplane in a gale. In Doncaster, where the weather was dreadful, instead of flying his huge biplane, Cody took an oath of allegiance before the town clerk in front of 50,000 spectators so that he could enter the *Daily Mail's* prize for flying a circular mile as a British subject.

The *Daily Mail* prizes determined the complexion of British aviation over the next few years. Lord Northcliffe, the newspaper's proprietor, was a passionate advocate of flight and frequently took the British government to task for its passive attitude to aviation. His challenges both created news and stimulated innovation. The cash prizes were significant, but taking part

ARTHUR W. BURGESS

TOP: The eventual winner of the London–Manchester race, Claude Graham-White, has to delay take-off due to the number of spectators gathered to see him off at Wormwood Scrubs. BOTTOM: Louis Blériot with his wife Alice before his departure on the successful Channel crossing attempt, on the front cover of *The Sphere*, 31 July 1909. OPPOSITE: Louis Paulhan outpaces a steam train in the London–Manchester air race, as depicted in *The Sphere*, 7 May 1910.

in the competitions also brought pilots and aeroplane builders fame and, in due course, sponsorship opportunities. Prizes were won by the prominent French aviators Louis Paulhan and Henri Farman. Some of these prizes were restricted to British contestants, and they secured successful careers for A. V. Roe, Claude Grahame-White and John Moore-Brabazon in designing aircraft and flying. Aviation goals were set by Northcliffe and achieved: the model aeroplane to fly furthest was designed by A. V. Roe; the first Channel crossing was flown by Louis Blériot; the first non-stop flight between London and Manchester was made by Paulhan; and the first 'Circuit of Britain' was flown by André Beaumont.

In the well-worn tradition of spectating aeronautical events, the launches of these races drew tens of thousands. Between 30,000 and 40,000 were present at the beginning of the 'Circuit of Britain' race in 1911. Its winner, Jean Conneau, who flew as André Beaumont, wrote a memoir the following year featuring crowds as a motif. In the Paris–Rome race of 1911 the roads and country lanes around the starting aerodrome near Versailles were thronged with people camping out in order to witness the race. Upon arrival in Rome Beaumont was accosted by 'an enthusiastic crowd, frantic with pleasure':

> I was lifted out of my seat and carried shoulder high. I had become their property and was unable either to utter a word or protect myself. Tossed about, dragged in every direction, I felt bruised and sore by the contact of thousands of hands trying to touch me, whilst wild shouts were filling the air.[28]

Having won the 'Circuit of Britain', Beaumont was lavishly feted at aviation-themed banquets and at film and music hall shows. He confessed that the last day of his junket was harder than flying the circuit: taken to the Crystal Palace for another banquet, he was spotted in the Sweet Pea exhibition and mobbed by a crowd of 2,000. Spectators at the public banquet thronged to touch him for good luck; having been smuggled out of the Palace, he was put on a train back to London which stopped at every station so that those waiting on the platform could shake his hand through the window.

Just as Pilâtre de Rozier had had his green coat torn to shreds by euphoric witnesses of his descent in the Montgolfière in 1783, so Wilbur Wright, André Beaumont and their competitors found themselves the

ABOVE: First National Aviation Meet, Indianapolis Motor Speedway, 13–18 June 1910.
BELOW: André Beaumont winning the Paris–Rome air race in 1911.

subjects of quite hysteric admiration across Europe in 1909–11. They were, for a short time, gods who had tamed the wind and achieved the impossible in their implausibly bulky yet flimsy planes. Their personal charisma mattered little; whether they were taciturn like Wright or voluble like Beaumont, the fact that they could master an aircraft and attain aviation milestones made them heroes, nowhere more so than in the pages of the newspapers that sponsored them.

The impact of these races was reflected not only in newsprint, but also on stage and screen and in the gate takings for airfields. Their newsworthiness brought flying into the cinemas, where many people had their first view of an aeroplane in flight in a newsreel item. The Hippodrome, Leicester Square, showed films from the same day's flying to contestants of the Circuit of Britain race in 1911 and, no doubt, to wider audiences in subsequent weeks – and at least 30,000 people had already witnessed the race's beginning at Brooklands. After a trip to the United States in 1909, the

ABOVE: '"Plane Fare". The Grand Stand of the Future', drawn by Alfred Leete for *The Sketch*, 6 October 1909. OPPOSITE: Detail from a London Underground poster for the Hendon Aerodrome, 1913 or 1914.

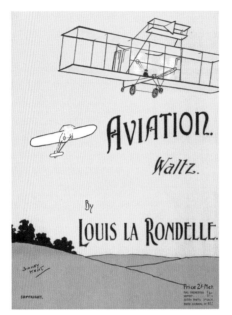

TOP LEFT: 'Aviation Waltz' by Louis La Rondelle, 1910. TOP RIGHT: 'Come Josephine in My Flying Machine (Up She Goes!)', by Fred Fischer, New York, *c*.1910. BOTTOM LEFT: 'The Aero Girl' by Julian Edwards, New York & London, *c*.1910. BOTTOM RIGHT: 'Aeroplane Valse' by Violet King, London, 1909.

aviator Claude Grahame-White noted the lucrative nature of stunt flying and set about turning Hendon Aerodrome, where he had based his flying operations and aircraft factory, into a popular attraction. His associates in the venture were Louis Blériot and Sir Hiram Maxim. It opened every weekend for rallies and stunt shows, with pilots performing jazz-inspired twists and turns in the air. There were concrete links with stage entertainment, from the novelty of booking a seat at Hendon by telephone from a leading West End box office to the many songs and dance numbers inspired by flight. The songs, untroubled by mechanical reality, continued to riff on an uncomplicated idea of flight as escape or romantic catalyst (e.g., 'Up in Your Old Biplane' or 'My Little Loving Aeroman', both 1912). Harry Tate performed a music hall sketch about the prize-winning frenzy of pioneer aviators in 1909. The first woman to fly the Channel, Harriet Quimby, had been a theatre critic and film scenario writer in her native United States. In 1913 and 1914 music hall artists collaborated on shows at Hendon, several of them flying planes themselves.

For all its spectacle and West End tie-ins, aviation was perhaps falling short of the very high expectations held at the turn of the century. Aeroplanes were not carrying people to the moon. They were barely lifting two passengers, and the maximum altitude achieved before mid 1909 was 500 feet. The somatic effects of aviation, which had been little considered before 1903, were beginning to manifest themselves. Air display audiences complained of 'aviation neck' after spending hours looking upwards. While members of the public had very little opportunity to experience aeroplane flight themselves before the First World War, there were some indications of the bodily impact of powered flight. From 1906 day trippers to Blackpool, Southport and New Brighton could take a spin in Sir Hiram Maxim's Captive Flying Machine, which had evolved as part of Maxim's aerodynamics research; his assistant reports 'a mighty mental struggle' before blacking out when being spun to 6G in a prototype: 'I recovered consciousness at about 3G, and was able to walk when we stopped.'[29] In 1913 a French pilot perfected looping the loop, instituting a new craze in stunt flying which was pioneered in Britain by B. C. Hucks. A photographic portrait of Hucks by the German-born British photographer Emil Otto Hoppé was used to endorse a new tranquillizer, Phosferine, after he professed that his 'nerves were becoming shaken' by flying.

In this period, passengers were being photographed in their hundreds in the cockpits of some fairly implausible aircraft. The painters who travelled between studios providing sets and backdrops for portrait photography were not much bothered by verisimilitude. Nor apparently were the clients who crowded over the wings: couples, family groups, gangs of young friends, gazing studiously at the camera, their Edwardian head-wear unruffled by the slip winds. Aeroplanes were just one option in an array of novelty vehicles, but by associating themselves with this new technology the photographed subjects were participating in flight as an idea, a practice and a pursuit. These portraits are just as meaningful as the vast numbers of shots of aviators poised for ascent in their fragile machines that appeared in the newspapers of the time.

ABOVE: *Flucht aus der Sandwüste* [Flight from the sand desert (i.e. military camp)], Neuhammer, Austria *c.*1910–12. OPPOSITE: Studio photograph with aeroplane. OVERLEAF: Studio photograph of Ruth Cavendish-Bentinck and Hermione Ramsden (the author's great great aunt), *c.*1912.

Aerial Warfare

By R. P. Hearne

With An Introduction by
SIR HIRAM S. MAXIM

> Civilization is to be undone and all our methods
> upset. The age of iron will be over, and the air-quake
> begun. … Humanity will learn how to control and
> deal with the 'nightmare of the future' when it will
> be possible to lay Paris, Berlin or London in a heap
> of smoking ruins before breakfast.
> – *South Wales Echo* (22 May 1909)[30]

As inventors moved ever closer to powered flight in the late nineteenth century, writers had considered the implications of aviation for the future. From the 1880s novels by George Griffith, Harry Collingwood, E. Douglas Fawcett and H. G. Wells in Britain, Jules Verne and Emile Driant in France, and Rudolf Martin in Germany offered many scenarios in which one individual or a country's commitment to, and development of, air power might alter the balance of international politics with devastating effect. This was not at the expense of more light-hearted imaginings of the potential of flight for human relationships: having published the bombastic *Angel of the Revolution*, which featured total war and successful aerial terrorism, in 1893, George Griffith went on to write *A Honeymoon in Space* (1901), in which an American heroine is taken on a sojourn from earth by her aristocratic British husband, encountering wonders of the kind previously imagined by Edgar Allan Poe and Richard Adams Locke.

But, as new geopolitical configurations were emerging, it was the martial potential of airships and aeroplanes that caught the popular imagination. In 1909 an 'air-quake' was announced, not by H. G. Wells or George Griffith, but by the editor of a regional British newspaper. Aircraft were spotted not only in the environs of air shows and races, but also by many residents of coastal towns, who reported seeing large inflatables coming from the direction of Germany. The phantom airship scare of 1909 was relished by some in Germany. Though no such sorties had been planned or executed, the Zeppelin did constitute a symbol of national strength that

TOP LEFT: Cover of *A Honeymoon in Space* by George Griffith, 1901. TOP RIGHT: Illustration by F. T. Janes for George Griffith's *The Angel of the Revolution*, 1893. In a new world war, an international terrorist Brotherhood intervenes from the air in an attack on London by Russian, French and Italian troops. BOTTOM: Illustration by F. T. Janes for George Griffith's *The Angel of the Revolution*, 1893. The Brotherhood's *Ithuriel* airship delivers the people of the United States from their corrupt government. PAGE 106: Cover of *Aerial Warfare* by R. P. Hearne, 1909.

complemented the state's newly consolidated navy, another source of discomfort for the British.

Just as the British Naval League had been founded in the 1890s in response to Kaiser Wilhelm's ambitions to surpass Britain's sea power, in January 1909 the Aerial League of the British Empire was formed. Made up of political, military and industrial figures and chaired by Lord Montagu of Beaulieu, the Aerial League agitated for greater government spending on air power, and set out to make the nation more 'air-minded'. Fundraisers were organized and promotional literature prepared. A song was commissioned which articulates the fears that led to the League's foundation:

When wooden walls and straining sails bore Britain's flag afar,
The nation prospered well in peace and feared no foe in war.
For Britain's might was everywhere and ruled the endless waves
Proclaiming to the world at large 'We never shall be slaves'.

And when the iron-clad replaced the ships that caught the breeze,
Britannia still retained her throne upon the charted seas.
For frowning fleets and giant guns outnumbered two to one,
The navies of all other lands beneath the sov'reign sun.

And now that every cloud conceals a lurking bird of prey,
Which threatens our supremacy in peace and war today,
Britannia must be equal to the peril and prepare
To hold our empire sacred from these dreadnoughts of the air.

Chorus: Britannia must rule the air as still she rules the sea.
To guard this realm beyond compare and keep her people free.
Britannia, Britannia must like the eagle be.[31]

Another less fear-mongering approach was taken by Grahame-White, who had the slogan 'Wake Up, England' painted onto a seaplane and overflew 121 towns on the south coast in 1912. In June the same year he scattered London with rose petals for Alexandra Day. He was advertising for the Hendon Aerodrome, which drew Londoners to north London to spectate and occasionally participate in flight. Patriotic, private and commercial interests merged in his programming of the venue, with Grahame-White's partners ranging from West End entertainers to members of the

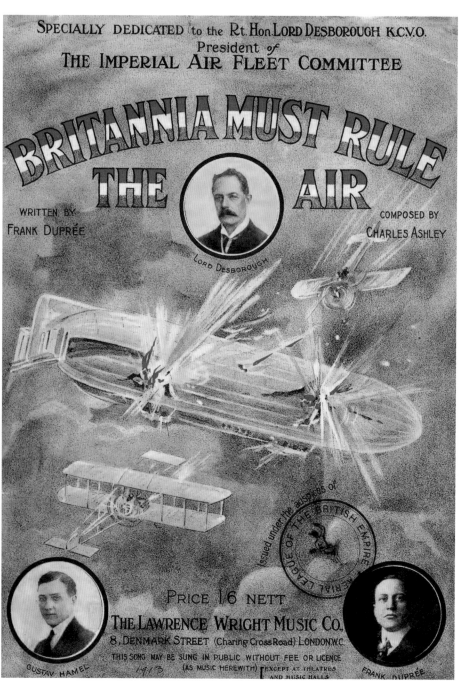

ABOVE: Aerial League song, 'Britannia Must Rule The Air', *c.*1913.
OPPOSITE: Claude Grahame-White depicted in a *Vanity Fair* supplement, 10 May 1911.

Parliamentary Aerial Defence Committee. He argued that it was by entertaining, rather than educating, that the importance of aviation would be effectively transmitted to the public. His air displays were aimed at cultivating a general interest that was 'not fickle or short-lived but sound and enduring ... by showing people what the aeroplane can do, thus teaching them the danger of neglecting aerial armament'.[32] To this end, spectators at a night derby were thrilled by illuminated aeroplanes mimicking dogfights, before bombarding a mock battleship built in the centre of the airfield. Grahame-White was probably unaware that he had recreated a scene from 1790s Paris, when balloons bombed a model of an English warship on the Champs de Mars in a fervour of nationalistic wish fulfilment.

Together with Harry Harper, the *Daily Mail*'s first aviation correspondent and an ever-present voice in the annals of early powered flight, Grahame-White also authored books for boys such as *With the Airmen* (1913) and, during the war, *Heroes of the Flying Corps* (1916). They were tapping into a fertile market. Air stories featured heavily in the 'juveniles', papers aimed at young boys from the mid 1890s. Several prominent airmen – Grahame-White himself, Alberto Santos-Dumont and Geoffrey

THE INVISIBLE
WAR-PLANE

CLAUDE
GRAHAME-
WHITE
AND
HARRY
HARPER

ABOVE LEFT: *With the Airmen* by Claude Grahame-White and Harry Harper, 1913.
ABOVE RIGHT: *Heroes of the Flying Corps* by Claude Grahame-White and Harry
Harper, 1916. OPPOSITE: *The Invisible War-Plane* by Claude Grahame-White and
Harry Harper, 1915.

de Havilland – declared their interest in aviation to have been sparked by
reading Verne as a child; H. G. Wells was also a potent influence. The new
generation of European men was growing up infused with the imaginative
potential of flight, aware of its dark side and ready to pursue the 'conquest
of the air' as its forefathers had striven for king and empire.

Despite the broad public interest, the British government was reluctant
to invest in aviation. The war minister's hand was forced in the foundation
of the Royal Flight Corps (RFC) in 1912 and the Royal Naval Air Service
(RNAS) in 1914, but progress in building up military aviation was slow until
several years after the outbreak of war. The RFC took a somewhat shabby
collection of sixty-three aeroplanes to France to support the British Expe-
ditionary Front in August 1914. As geographical deadlock set in at the end
of 1914, the Corps' role became key, for it allowed for a view over enemy
lines in order to direct artillery fire and discern troop movements. But pilots
and the newly created 'observers' were unfamiliar with the northern French
terrain and found it difficult to reconnoitre effectively. The first Allied air
raids were carried out that autumn on Zeppelin bases in Germany, and
from the spring of 1915 there were retaliatory Zeppelin raids on Britain, in
a ghastly realization of the airship scare years earlier.

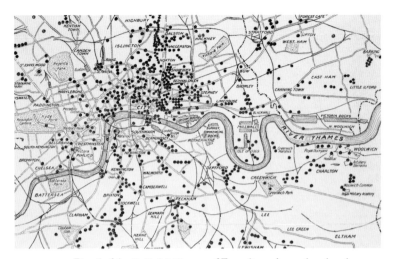

ABOVE: Detail of the *Daily Mail*'s map of Zeppelin and aeroplane bombs on London, 31 January 1919. OPPOSITE: Neighbours examine part of a bomb dropped by a Zeppelin in 1915. Photograph by H. D. Girdwood.

The German public's pride in the Zeppelin stood in great contrast to British nervousness in the pre-war years. The Zeppelin was feted by the German government from 1908, but it also stood as a symbol of popular sovereignty, given Count Zeppelin's disdain for authority and bureaucracy. When one of the airships burst at Echterdingen in 1908, its rebuild was funded by public subscription. Zeppelin souvenirs abounded, from miniatures to postcards, and world domination seemed to beckon, with a board game which moved Zeppelins across the globe. After the First World War the British artist Solomon J. Solomon, who was convinced that German camouflage operations had deceived Allied reconnaissance interpreters, contended that the Zeppelin's passenger service had intentionally made civilians conversant with the unfamiliar aerial view of the ground in order to train better *camofleurs*.

Much confidence was placed in Zeppelins at the outbreak of war, and there were celebrations around Germany at the news of the first night attacks on London in September 1915. In fact these did little damage initially, but they had a heavy psychological impact on the British population. Repeated attacks over 1916 and 1917, in concert with Gotha bomber planes, killed and injured hundreds of people. Defence against such attacks consisted of 'pom-pom' anti-aircraft guns, which were hard to handle and often of

TOP: Stereoscopic photograph of the Graf Zeppelin in Egypt, 1931.
BOTTOM: Postcard of the German dirigible Hansa arriving at Potsdam harbour.
OPPOSITE: A pull-out model of a Zeppelin, included in *The Highway of the Air: An Illustrated Record of Aviation*, August 1909.

The Highway of the Air

An Illustrated Record of Aviation

SUPPORTING PLANE

R.E.H.P. ANZANI MOTOR
PROPELLER

VERTICAL RUDDER
AIR CHAMBER
TELESCOPIC JOINT

AVIATOR'S SEAT
ELEVATING PLANE
WHEELS SUPPORTING MONOPLANE ON GROUND
SUPPORTING PLANE

M. BLÉRIOT'S FRENCH MONOPLANE
on which he performed the first
CALAIS-DOVER FLIGHT, 25th JULY, 1909

Including a Dissectible Model of the

ZEPPELIN AIRSHIP

FUNK & WAGNALLS COMPANY
August 1909

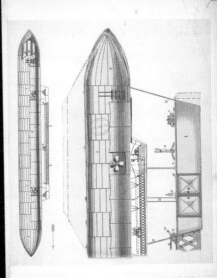

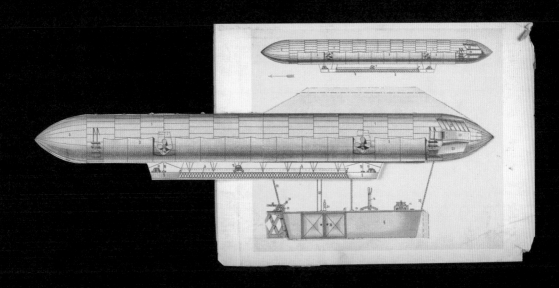

118

TOP: British recruitment poster, 1914–18. The small number of casualties from bombing in the First World War, relative to that of the front line, proved that it was in fact far safer to stay at home than to 'face the bullets' at the battlefront. BOTTOM: The downed L32 airship in Essex, 1916. Photograph by C. H. Girdwood.

insufficient range, and acetylene searchlights installed around the capital and other cities and ports. The development of incendiary bullets in September 1916 made it possible to shoot down the Zeppelins (normal bullets were ineffective in bursting the gasbags). These downings met with exultation, giving south-easterners an occasional moment of triumph amidst their anxiety over aerial attacks. When the German L32 airship was destroyed at Billericay in Essex on 25 September, the *Times* correspondent had 'never seen the like of it as a holiday of national rejoicing'.[33] Thousands flocked to the scene, filling trains and abandoning vehicles in country lanes to view 'an immense tangle of twisted metal, girders, machinery ... like the skeleton of a monstrous prehistoric reptile, the aluminium girders, corroded by fire, suggesting its bleached bones'.[34] Locals in their hundreds picked through the potato fields for souvenir scraps to sell. A week later the feat was repeated with the L31, which was watched by hundreds of thousands of Londoners. The same correspondent was walking home over Black-friars Bridge:

> Looking up the clear run of New Bridge Street and Farringdon Road I saw high in the sky a concentrated blaze of searchlights and in its centre a ruddy glow which rapidly spread into the outline of a burning airship. Then the searchlights were turned off and the Zeppelin drifted perpendicularly in the darkened sky, a gigantic pyramid of flames, red and orange, like a ruined star falling slowly to earth. Its glare lit up the streets and gave a ruddy tint even to the waters of the Thames.
>
> The spectacle lasted two or three minutes. It was so horribly fascinating that I felt spell-bound – almost suffocated with emotion, ready hysterically to laugh or cry. When at last the doomed airship vanished from sight there arose a shout of mingled execration, triumph and joy; a swelling shout that appeared to be rising from all parts of the metropolis, ever increasing in force and intensity.[35]

The airship fell to the ground in Hertfordshire as locals sang the national anthem. Over the following days the wreck exerted an attraction similar to that of the L32 in Essex.

Back on the Western Front, 1915 saw more effective photographic recon-naissance and planes equipped with guns. The balance tipped over the year from German to Allied advantage as new types of aeroplanes were rushed

into service, both for reconnaissance and to attack in the air. By mid 1916 several German, French and British pilots had made a name for themselves during daring aerial combat. Their exploits were seized upon by newspapers looking for a human angle that contrasted with the miserably slow progress of trench-bound infantry and dreadful battle casualty counts, and the Ace was born. The United States' entry into the war in 1917 brought more names to the roster. The pilots, almost all of whom died in combat, were glorified as national heroes, and their photographs and interviews disseminated widely. David Lloyd George made them the subject of a speech in the House of Commons in 1917: 'The heavens are their battlefields; they are the Cavalry of the clouds ... Their daily, yea, their nightly struggles, are like the Miltonic conflict between the winged hosts of light and darkness'.[36] Meanwhile, in Italy the writer Gabriele D'Annunzio, who organized and led missions to bomb Austrian cities with ammunition and propaganda leaflets, produced similarly hyperbolic prose about his countrymen's affinity for the air.

The aces generated a great deal of newsprint and memoirs during and immediately after the war. Many British airmen went on afterwards to testify, quietly, that wartime flying had been a terrifying and confusing experience. Norman Macmillan, an RFC lieutenant who went on to become an aviation writer and test pilot, remembered:

We were continually on the alert against the enemy whom we had to fight. We had to look in front of us, above us, around us, behind us and below us. We had to develop an entirely new sense of sight, of vision, the enemy might be anywhere. On the ground the enemy was ahead, in the air he might be anywhere. We had to live a life within a sphere instead of a life that was horizontal on the ground.[37]

Even William Johns, who would go on to create the most influential fictional airman of the twentieth century, Biggles, admitted that the air action was considerably less exciting and glamorous than contemporary written reports would have it. As a counterpart to Lloyd George's excited rhetoric, we might turn to the 1919 poem by W. B. Yeats's 'An Irish Airman Foresees his Death'. Yeats's pilot is driven not by patriotism or glory:

> Nor law, nor duty bade me fight,
> Nor public man, nor cheering crowds,
> A lonely impulse of delight
> Drove to this tumult in the clouds.

ABOVE: A line-up of German aces, with designer Myn Heir Fokker on top left, from *King of Air Fighters* by James Ira Thomas Jones, 1934. OPPOSITE: 'Princess Shakhovskaya, The First Military Airwoman'. Having learnt to fly in Germany, this aristocrat was accepted as an aerial scout by the Russian Flying Corps. *The Sketch*, 9 December 1914.

ABOVE: 'Our valiant aviators in aerial combat', French postcard, *c.*1915.
OPPOSITE: Looking up from the German trenches. From *Simplicissimus*,
22 December 1914.

His indifference to the grand forces at play beyond his cockpit, and his disregard for and even boredom with his own life, lead him to engage in aerial combat. Elements of this character – the cool deliberation, the drive away from social ties – would go on to constitute the stereotype of the interwar airman.

As well as 'engaging' enemy pilots in aerial combat, armed aeroplanes were used to attack ground troops – the pilot or observer using the machine gun to 'strafe,' or mow, the ground indiscriminately. Little wonder then that, as with the Zeppelin, the aeroplane exerted a psychological effect beyond its individual firepower. RFC Commander Trenchard complained in 1916 that

> the mere presence of a hostile machine in the air inspires those on the ground with exaggerated forebodings with regard to what the machine is capable of doing. For instance, at one time on one part of the front, whenever a hostile machine, or what was thought to be a hostile machine, was reported, whistles were blown and men hid in the trenches.[38]

Yet terror was not the only inspiration of the aeroplanes flying over the line – hope, admiration and the fantasy of escaping upwards from the ghastly mire of the trenches was also provoked by the sight of an aircraft, the spectacle of a dogfight and the prospect of seeing an enemy downed.

ABOVE: Pilots evade searchlights in this night training exercise depicted in *The Modern Boy's Book of Aircraft*, 1931. OPPOSITE: 'Dog Fight. Knights of the Air!' Cover of *The Modern Boy*, 9 January 1932.

The war made an arena of the sky. For the first time it was habitual to look and listen upwards, for both enemy and friendly aircraft. The new reality of attack from the air was recognized and legislated for with stringent blackout rules. 'The Zeppelin scare is just as if the whole place was in imminent fear of an earthquake', reported an Australian general on leave. 'At night the whole of London is in absolute darkness, every window heavily screened, no street lamps, no lamps on vehicles, all trains with windows closed and blinds drawn, constant street accidents and traffic blocks, and a bewildering pandemonium of confusion in the streets'.[39] The searchlights that accompanied anti-aircraft guns, shining beams up into the sky, looked all the more striking in contrast to the darkness, and their visual impact was recorded by artists and photographers for postcards. Airspace over likely targets, such as ports and factories, was further occupied by barrage balloons, kite balloons that were tethered with sharpened steel cables capable of slicing off an aeroplane's wing if it passed too close.

All these elements served to draw the eye upwards, and this new attention remained after the war. In her 1925 novel *Mrs Dalloway* Virginia Woolf chose an aeroplane, whose noise on first appearance 'bored ominously into the ears of the crowd', to unite the attention of a disparate selection of Londoners, and to evoke with precision the post-war responses to flight of both apprehension and exhilaration.

· MOTHS ·
IN
PUBLIC SERVICE

THE
Royal Air Force.

BRISTOL

HANTS

6   The Joy of the Ride

Peace. Nothing more to destroy. So aviation
becomes unemployed.
– Le Corbusier, *Aircraft* (1935)[40]

In its first decade in Europe, powered flight had gone from being a sport
to constituting a war industry. British production of aircraft and training of personnel, which had initially been very slow and piecemeal, had
reached a steady and efficient level by the time the war ended in 1918.
The Royal Air Force (RAF), formed in March 1918 from the RFC and the
RNAS, was the world's largest air force, with over 22,000 aeroplanes, 103
airships and almost 700 aerodromes. There were now a significant number
of people who had worked in aviation: tens of thousands of pilots had
been instructed; over 200,000 men had trained as mechanics, ground staff
and aerial photography operatives; and around 347,000 Britons (of whom
over one-third were women) were working in aircraft manufacture. But
an aviation industry at this scale was unsustainable in peacetime. Airmen
were decommissioned, factories closed and workers, in particular women,
laid off. Grahame-White's premises at Hendon were retained for use as a
government airbase. The RAF struggled to justify its continued existence, but
found a role in the air policing of new British mandates such as Palestine
and Iraq. Civil aviation, decided Air Minister Winston Churchill, 'must fly
by itself; our Government cannot possibly hold it up in the air'.[41]

    In some ways the government's withdrawal of support left things where
they had been before the war. Once more flying was the preserve of the
wealthy or those who could secure sponsorship from the manufacturers.
Once again minds were put to fulfilling *Daily Mail* challenges, such as
the non-stop Atlantic crossing for which Northcliffe had offered £10,000

in 1913. But certain things had changed. The government's excess stock of aeroplanes, already far more reliable than pre-war models, was auctioned off at £5 a plane at Hendon, cheaper by half than the mechanic's charge for its certificate of airworthiness. Excellent aerial cameras were also available to buy. For the enterprising ex-RAF staff who could draw on some capital, it was a simple matter to obtain several machines and accessories in order to explore the possibilities of civil flying.

The public attitude to flight had also changed. It was clear that death was easily come by in an aeroplane and, for all the morale-boosting properties of the cult of the aces, it showed the sky to be an arena of danger. People were rattled by hearing planes and seeing airships overhead after the terrifying experience of aerial bombardment up and down the country. Aviation was tainted by war, and it took some effort by those who sought to benefit from peacetime flying to rehabilitate it.

Within seven months of the Armistice, transatlantic flight had been achieved by Captains John Alcock and Arthur Brown in a converted Vickers Vimy bomber, which, without its munitions, could carry sufficient petrol for the range of the flight. This was followed by a series of long-distance races across the British Empire, funded by colonial governments, which succeeded in creating a new hype around the veteran airmen, all flying

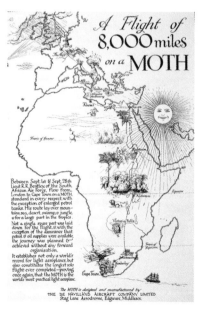

ABOVE: The Sir Ross Smith Aeroplane Race Game, 1920s. OPPOSITE LEFT: Report
of John Alcock and Arthur Brown's Atlantic crossing on the front cover of *The Daily
Mirror*, 14 June 1919. OPPOSITE RIGHT: 'A Flight of 8,000 miles on a Moth.' Map of
Capt. R. R. Bentley's London–Cape Town flight, from *Airways* magazine, 1928.
PAGE 126: De Havilland Moths in Public Service. Cover of *Airways* magazine, May 1928.

converted bombers. These men and their machines, no longer in the service
of death, were rather connecting Britain with its newly expanded territories. There was a great deal of appetite for the exploits and anecdotes of
these journeys. Captain Ross Smith, who won the London–Australia race
with his brother, presented his recollections of the flight in a multimedia
travelogue show in both Sydney and London, with the help of good publi-
cists, the Australian photographer Captain Frank Hurley and the American
journalist Lowell Thomas. Smith's account of the journey was published in
1922, after he had died in an air crash. An extract from the publicity for his
Australian show provides a sense of the kind of attraction being offered to
audiences:

> You'll see one-half of the globe spinning beneath your feet – cities,
> towns, rivers, mountain peaks – all strange to you, yet brought so
> close you feel like reaching out and touching them. You'll almost
> feel the insufferable heat as the Vimy ploughs her way through

the skies above the steaming deserts – you'll shiver, even as the 'men who did it' might have, as you are entrapped in the drenching, torrential rains of the Near East – you'll clench your teeth and hang tight to the seat as the giant 'plane swoops, dives and swirls through the vast open spaces of the air route – and you'll taste, too, the thrill of pride that must have been theirs when they landed victorious in the Australia that gave them birth.[42]

Audiences are offered a somatic experience, a chance to feel what the aviators felt as they flew. The extreme sensations are linked to the wider theme of patriotism, with the adverse conditions presented not by enemy fire but by the weather. Once again, there is a strong sense of the air as something to be conquered and subdued.

Proponents of peacetime aviation focused on its utility in communications between Britain and its collection of unevenly dispersed territories. As well as linking the Empire, aviation was providing a mirror to it in the form of aerial photography. The skills built up during wartime reconnaissance were put to use by the same cohort of ex-RAF airmen and photography experts. Aerofilms, founded in 1919, began photographing notable British cities and sites from the air and sold these photographs to newspapers, postcard printers, encyclopedias and the proprietors of the sites themselves. As late as the 1970s Aerofilms sales agents were knocking on doors offering householders a photographic view of their homes from above. Companies were formed in Africa and the Far East to undertake photographic mapping and boundary, forestry, and geographical surveys on behalf of governments and prospectors. The regular publication of photographs by these companies in illustrated newspapers involved the readers vicariously in the regulation of overseas territories, for example by inviting them to scrutinize a photomap of a Sarawak jungle for signs of illegal plantations.

Opportunities to fly were growing. Many ex-RAF pilots set up passenger flying operations. Major Jack Savage equipped a surplus S.E.5 biplane with oil-filled exhaust pipes and began offering companies the chance to have their product names written in the sky. While a few companies focused on transportation, most were in the business of short novelty flights called 'joyrides', or stunt flying shows inspired by 'barnstorming' set-ups in the United States. In the early 1920s tens of thousands of passengers paid between 5 shillings and £1 (£14–£47 in today's money) to be taken up for a short flight by local companies around the British Isles. Quite remarkably,

TOP: 'Fearless Freddie', a Hollywood stuntman about to drop from an aeroplane into an automobile, 10 November 1921. BOTTOM: Looping the loop over London in an Avro biplane. From *The Sphere*, 14 June 1919.

Detail from a colour lithograph by Charles G. Dickson advertising the Imperial
Airways Cairo-Baghdad-Karachi service, 1924. The Pyramids are brought
into visual correspondence with Baghdad and the Himalayas in the wake of
an Armstrong Whitworth Argosy airliner.

no members of the public were killed (though there were frequent fatalities in display flying). Alan Cobham, a former RFC pilot who ran one of these companies and who went on to dominate the joyriding market in the 1930s, asserted that, by making the British public air-minded, he and his colleagues were doing the country a great service:

> The coming generation will think aviationally and will take to flying as an everyday means of progression. As for those poor souls of the present and past generations who still look upon it with awe, as some dangerous adventure, and who will not be converted, we, in aviation can only wait for their latter end, hoping that in the meantime, if they do not help us, at least they will not hinder us.[43]

By putting flight within the reach of many ordinary people, aviators were certainly making it less frightening. A souvenir postcard publicizing Psyche's Circus, the venture of Mr H. Sykes, showed a picture of one Mrs Sissons in cap and goggles with a mirthful expression, accompanied by the ditty:

> Over the ground and up you go!
> With 'Psyche' on the gay wind's wing;
> Some are afraid, but why be so,
> When Mrs Sissons aged One-o-one
> So merrily takes the Flight and the Fling
> With only a thought for the fun of the thing,
> And the joy of courting her Aerial King?
> So jump to the chance of being a bird –
> Book now for the honour of saying 'I dared'.[44]

Concurrent with the spread of joyriding operations was the growth in the number of point-to-point flights offered by companies from 1919. Passenger services were offered between London and Paris and, in the space of a year between 1921 and 1922, 5,000 people travelled this way. In 1924 Imperial Airways was set up with a state subsidy as the national carrier from the combined fleets and pilots of four private airlines. Regular services to India and South Africa were not achieved until the very end of the decade, but, regardless, Imperial Airways publicity created a sense of air connections between disparate parts of the Empire, as a 1924 poster shows.

ABOVE: Detail from the front cover of *Airways* magazine, June 1928.
OPPOSITE: Detail from 'Anticipation and Realisation': a cartoon by
Charles G. Dickson from *Airways* magazine, February 1926.

Airline companies were very unlikely to present flight as something daring, but rather emphasized the regular reliability of their aeroplanes and the safety and comfort of air travel. Women were targeted particularly on the assumption that if a woman was not afraid to fly, a man would not be either. National airlines sponsored passenger-centred magazines, precursors of the in-flight magazine, that were aimed as much at women as at male enthusiasts of flight. In its first issue the British publication *Airways* included a feature by Harry Harper on the calm bearing of female air passengers in contrast to the demeanour of men. In cartoons and other sketches, a young modern woman is used as a foil to a middle-aged man who is suspicious about flying. A 1932 brochure entitled 'Special Notes to Ladies on Air Travel' asserts that 'it is easier to look charming after an air journey than by any other form of travel', given the on-board lavatory and the 'absence' of dust and dirt. Special air travel outfits were soon designed and marketed in the pages of *Airways*, a recurring item being fur coats in those days of uninsulated cabins.

In contrast to the unctuous rhetoric of advertising copy, passenger flying was a dirty, noisy and uncomfortable business in its early decades, as well as being extremely expensive. The converted DH34 biplanes used in the 1920s were fitted out with eight wicker chairs, the only concession to cosiness being a measure of chintz upholstery. On some Continental airlines, but not in Britain, passengers were given earplugs. Fatalities were high, and insurers initially refused to cover passengers who chose to fly (the airline certainly could not). From this point of view it is remarkable that Imperial Airways' passenger numbers grew at all through the 1920s, from 10,000 a year in 1924 to 28,000 in 1929, increasing to over 50,000 in the late 1930s.

By the late 1920s aeroplane travel had been absorbed into the identity of an outward-looking, imperial Britain. While it may not have replaced

ABOVE: Alan Cobham departs from the River Medway in a Short military flying boat, Singapore I, for a route survey of Africa, 17 November 1927. OPPOSITE: Short's next model of flying boat, the Calcutta, was used for passenger services from the Mediterranean to India from the late 1920s. From *The Modern Boy's Book of Aircraft*, 1931.

seafaring, it certainly vied with it for eyecatching visuals and salty anecdotes. While flight itself, especially with a destination other than the originating airfield, was still out of reach for the great majority, the sights and sensations of flight were becoming more and more widely described, from newspaper accounts and photographs to newsreels or feature films at the cinema (18 million Britons went to the cinema every week). Alan Cobham garnered industry and government support to survey imperial routes. He took a British Gaumont cameraman with him to document these flights and showed the footage on his lecture tours, later releasing feature films such as *With Cobham to the Cape* and *Round Africa with Cobham* (the former was re-released, with some of the casual racism expunged, in 1976).

Cobham's reliability made him the most famous pilot of the period and he was well placed to find sponsors for his various initiatives to 'Get Britain Flying'. In 1929 he worked with Lord Wakefield to take 10,000 schoolchildren on free aeroplane rides, as well as 40,000 paying passengers. Altogether one-quarter of a million spectators attended the twenty-one airfields in his 'Youth of Britain' tour. In the following years he launched National Aviation Days, a joint air show and joyride outfit that toured Britain and South Africa and became known, fondly but against his will,

Entirely New!

SIR ALAN
COBHAM'S

NATIONAL AVIATION　　　　DAY　CAMPAIGN

AIR
DISPLAY

SAT. & SUN.
JULY
13 & 14
FOR TWO DAYS ONLY

KIRKCALDY
CHAPEL FARM, LOCHGELLY ROAD
Continuous 2-30 p.m. till dusk.　Two Complete Displays 2-30 and 6-30 p.m.
SPECIAL CHILDREN'S HOUR 5-30 TO 6-30 P.M.
ADMISSION 1/3.　CHILDREN 6d.　CARS 1/-.　FLIGHTS FROM 4/-
SPECIAL AUGMENTED BUS SERVICES TO AND FROM THE FLYING GROUND.

LEARN
TO FLY
ON A
DE HAVILLAND
"MOTH"

AT THE
DE HAVILLAND SCHOOL OF FLYING,
STAG LANE AERODROME, EDGWARE, MIDDLESEX.

ABOVE: Advertisement for Moth flying lessons, from *Airways* magazine, 1926.
OPPOSITE: Poster for Sir Alan Cobham's National Aviation Day Air Display, 1929.

as 'Cobham's Flying Circus'. By the end of the decade Cobham calculated that he and his pilots had carried almost one million paying passengers, and that three million had bought tickets for the show.

The sense that a population familiar with and skilled in flying was desirable was slowly beginning to take hold in government circles. In 1925 the government had funded the creation of ten new light flying clubs around the country, subsidizing flying lessons and the cost of a commercial licence, to encourage more than the wealthy few to learn to pilot light aircraft such as the very popular Gipsy Moth. Even so, only 500 men possessed the licence in 1927, the same year that women were finally allowed to hold the licence and to fly for a living. Annual exhibitions and air shows continued to attract large audiences and to offer new ways for the public to engage with aeroplanes. Machines designed to test one's reflexes were put on show. The queue to try the Reid Pilot Indicator at the 1929 International Aero Exhibition at London's Olympia was so long, and so predominantly female, that a special time was set aside for women to test their skills. The prize of a free course of flying instruction at Hanworth Aerodrome was available to the two best entrants; it was given to a man and a woman, despite reports that the six female finalists scored higher than their six male counterparts.

'The Gateway to London: An Armstrong-Whitworth Argosy air-liner
in flight over the heart of the City.' Photograph by Capt. A. G. Buckham
published in *Airways* magazine, February 1928.

Memories of the war continued to cling to aviation. Virtually all American films featuring aeroplanes were about aerial combat on the Western Front, with *Wings* winning Best Picture at the first Academy Awards in 1927 and having a significant impact in British cinemas. While in some contexts it was shifting to a sunny post-war future, flight imagery also drew on a sublime register deriving from the drama of aerial warfare. Just as Captain Ross Smith was described as locked in conflict with the elements, the photographs of Captain Alfred G. Buckham, published in both aviation and mainstream journals in the 1920s, evoke a mortal engagement with the weather. Buckham had been seriously injured during his time in the RNAS, as a consequence of which he had to breathe through a tube in his throat and was unable to speak normally. But he produced sumptuous composite images of aeroplanes in flight over dappled landscapes and towering cloudscapes. The captions that often accompanied these images hinted at the hair-raising dangers he faced while taking the photographs as a solo pilot, his ankle tied to his seat and the rest of him hanging out of the aircraft to expose the plate.

The decisive moment of the transfiguration of flight from a war-tainted technology to a technology for the future was 1927, when Charles Lindbergh arrived in Paris after a 33-hour solo flight from Long Island, New York. This relatively unknown American pilot was too young to have fought in the war. With his Atlantic crossing he secured a $25,000 prize set up in 1919 by a Franco-American businessman, Raymond Orteig. For a few months he also became the most famous man in the world. Several teams of aviators had tried to undertake the Paris–New York non-stop journey (there was no requirement for it to be a solo flight), and only a fortnight before Lindbergh's success two famous French aviators, Captains François Coli and Charles Nungesser, had disappeared in the attempt. Unlike the American, both had been aces during the war, and they flew with Nungesser's lucky but somewhat morbid colours (a coffin and a skull and crossbones) painted on their plane. The triumph of the fresh-faced, 25-year-old New Worlder over the grizzled veterans, who were long mourned in France, marked both a beginning and an end. Lindbergh provided the first post-war template of a heroic pilot who had not come from military flying, and his hyperbolic reception marked the climax of a period of grand wonder around flight. A week after his arrival in Le Bourget, Lindbergh was feted by 500,000 Parisians on the capital's streets. As he approached Croydon Aerodrome by air, he found himself

ABOVE: Crowds greeting Lindbergh at Croydon, 1927. OPPOSITE: Lindbergh's
Spirit of St Louis on the Atlantic crossing. Illustration by Manning de V. Lee
in *Historic Airships* by R. Holland, 1928.

unable to land as 100,000 spectators surged onto the field. He was escorted
back up the coast of the United States in a convoy of dirigibles, aeroplanes
and destroyers before being driven past 4 million onlookers in New York.
Considering that the city's total population was only around 5 million, this
turn-out beat that for Charles and Robert's first manned gas balloon launch
in 1780s Paris, which was a mere half of that city's population (see page 34).

Star pilots continued to be celebrated, with special acclaim for female
pilots – who were always 'intrepid', such as the American Amelia Earhart
(even though her 1928 transatlantic flight had been made as a passenger).
Until the British aviator Amy Johnson scored a victory for the middle classes
with her astounding solo flight from England to Australia in 1930, almost all
the women in the cockpit had been (or had married) aristocrats. Their titles
made it all the easier for them to gain the headlines. Mary, Lady Heath,
an Irish Olympic athlete who was the first woman to gain a commercial
licence, undertook the first solo flight from Cape Town to London in 1928.
Lady Mary Bailey flew to Cape Town while the 'Flying Duchess', Mary
Russell, Duchess of Bedford, undertook several record-breaking long-
distance flights in 1929 and 1930.Johnson had learned to fly at weekends
while working as a typist and had gained the backing of the charismatic
director of civil aviation, Sir Sefton Brancker, in her venture to make a new
flight record. Not much was made of her departure but, as the days went

ABOVE: 'Amy', words by Jos. Geo. Gilbert, music by Horatio Nicholls, *c*.1930.
OPPOSITE: Amelia Earhart in a Stearman-Hammond Y1 monoplane, which won a
Department of Commerce competition for the safest and most practical aeroplane
under $700, 1936.

by and Johnson reported in from increasingly distant stopping points, her flight captured the national imagination and the news of her arrival in Darwin in May was celebrated around Britain. A song, 'Amy, wonderful Amy', was written in her honour which pointed out, 'Yesterday you were but a nonentity, now you will go down in posterity'. The transformational power of flying had been proven: skill, tenacity and a willingness to get oil on your hands could not only win one records, but could also make one as famous as a movie star. Framed portraits of Johnson were given away with girls' magazines so that they might have a new role model.

The more spectacular side of British aviation was provided by the RAF, which displayed a show of force annually at Hendon and on other special occasions. The register of these flying displays was unashamedly military, including stunts performed in a combat context and dive bombings of a mocked-up foreign seaport. In August 1928 Londoners in their thousands were treated to an invasion rehearsal, with the 'bombing' of the Air Ministry played out as a light show. Meanwhile civil aviation routes across the Empire were being reconnoitred and instituted. The ambition was to connect the metropolis with India, South Africa and Australia. In the 1920s airships seemed a more promising vehicle than aeroplanes for such long-distance flying and an Empire Communications Scheme got under way, backed by a combination of industry capital and government subsidy. Several successful

ABOVE: Front cover for a souvenir booklet on the Graff Zeppelin's world trip, *c.*1929.
OPPOSITE: The R100 moored at Cardington, 1938. PAGES 146–47: 'The London
Season, Hendon, the Air Pageant.' From the *Mayfair Hotel Book*, ed. C. Whitley, 1927.

Atlantic crossings, and a system of airship masts that would allow the vessels to moor and unload passengers, led at the end of the 1920s to confidence in the scheme coming to fruition.

Two airships were commissioned, the R100, to be built by Vickers, and the R101, to be built at the Royal Airship Works. Since the latter was supported by the Labour air minister Lord Thomson, they became known respectively as the capitalist airship and the socialist airship. Hangars and masts were erected at home and abroad in anticipation of the passenger service soon to be inaugurated. The R100 was received rapturously in Canada in the summer of 1930, and it returned triumphant. In October that year the R101 set out on an inaugural return flight to India, carrying Lord Thomson, Sir Sefton Brancker and dozens of journalists. Seven hours into the flight it crashed in bad weather and exploded near Beauvais, killing forty-eight passengers, including the ministers. The impact of this terrible incident has been compared to that of the *Titanic*, with the joint funeral procession drawing as many spectators as had attended the last coronation in 1911. Yet, while it drew a line under airships, the crash did not affect the take-up of aeroplane flight. Aviation was to become an increasingly important part of British national identity over the next two decades.

THE SHEIK

THE BUSINESS GIRL

THE SPORTSMAN

THE MESSENGER BO[Y]

THE BUSINESS   (Right)   THIS LADY, AGED 90,
MAN   FLIES TO AND FROM PARIS

Aerial Nationalism

> Aviation provided the great powers with their
> 'calling-cards'.
> – Peter Fritzsche, *A Nation of Fliers* (1992)[45]

The 1930s saw aviation deployed in myriad nation-building enterprises. Some of these were conceived and executed explicitly as shows of political might, while others operated within a context of nationalism but with different agendas. There was an effort in many countries to widen the appeal and understanding of aeroplane flight in order to be better equipped should war break out.

The pageantry that had accompanied flight from its beginnings continued to enthral and engage audiences. In Britain Alan Cobham's National Aviation Days toured the country, its mainly male team offering rides and aerial spectacles, as well as inspiration to hundreds of aspiring pilots. An anecdote claims that 75 per cent of candidates interviewed for the RAF in 1939 said they'd flown with Cobham. The public appetite for joyriding was high – for example, there were 92,000 passengers in 1932 – enough even to support rival outfits such as the British Hospitals Air Pageant, which was founded by several of Cobham's ex-associates. The air display at Hendon, which often culminated in the destruction of a topically themed enemy, was only the British iteration of a pan-European flexing of nationalist muscle. Italy's Days of the Wing drew Roman spectators to shows of force against mocked-up North African villages. The gatherings of members of the French nationalist Croix-de-Feu party began to feature fly-bys in the early 1930s, with thirty planes featuring in a 15,000-strong meeting in Oued-Smar, Algeria in 1935. In Germany, where domestic aviation capacity had been limited by the Treaty of Versailles, gliding rallies in the

ABOVE: Italian poster celebrating Italo Balbo's formation crossing of the Atlantic, 1933.
OPPOSITE: '6pm in London – 7pm in Le Touquet': front and inside of an Imperial
Airways brochure, early 1930s. PAGE 150: 'They All Fly',
page from *Popular Flying*, April 1932.

Wasserkuppe mountains drew 20,000 spectators. The rise to power of the
National Socialist Party was celebrated by a spectacular May Day rally
at Berlin's Tempelhof Airport in 1933, where aeroplanes, along with well-
choreographed masses of youths, provided a vision of the party's ambitious
future. Hitler's arrival by aeroplane at a 1934 rally in Nuremberg was used
to spectacular effect in the propaganda film he commissioned from Leni
Riefenstahl, *Triumph of the Will* (1935).

153

    The fascist fascination with aviation was also evident in Italy. Mussolini,
like Napoleon over a century earlier, found in flight a powerful aesthetic
tool and was a proponent of display flying. Having himself abandoned
flying lessons as his political career gathered momentum, he considered
air supremacy, and national air-mindedness, as key elements of his vision
for Italy. It was a vision shared by the futurist poet and agitator Filippo
Marinetti. Long inspired by the kinaesthetic sensations of flight, Marinetti
launched a new manifesto on *aeropittura*, or 'aeropainting', in 1928, celebrating the new framings of the world made possible by aviation. Meanwhile
Mussolini and his air minister Italo Balbo oversaw huge investment in a
fascist air force; as Balbo declared, 'the war-like spirit of our aviators is at
one with our Fascist soul'.[46] Balbo organized international mass flights to

showcase Italian air values. Sixty-one Savoia-Marchetti seaplanes flew in formation around the western Mediterranean in June 1928, undertaking another aerial 'cruise' to Odessa in 1929 to court the Soviet Union as a potential ally against western Europe. In 1930 Balbo orchestrated a formation crossing of the Atlantic to Rio de Janeiro, and in 1933 he led 100 airmen to New York. All the pilots wore black shirts beneath their flight suits, and their numbers and ability to fly in formation were signifiers of the facist message of group discipline. The aviators returned to Rome to a tremendous popular reception, with out-of-towners encouraged by the publicity and discount rail fares to travel to the capital for the occasion. Balbo was given unprecedented honours, but was then effectively exiled to the distant post of governor of Libya in case his feats made him more popular than Il Duce.

The British response to such grandiose flying was muted. Such a level of state financing of aviation was unthinkable; it was up to Imperial Airways, whose subsidy was paid by the government, to represent Britain's aerial prowess. With airships discredited after the terrible explosion at Beauvais in 1930 (see page 149), more money was made available for the airline's Empire-connecting routes; it gradually built airmail and passenger services

ABOVE LEFT: Poster for KLM, between 1931 and 1935. ABOVE RIGHT: PanAm timetable, September 1939. OPPOSITE: Imperial Airways England–South Africa timetable cover, July 1938. OVERLEAF: Imperial Airways England–South Africa timetable, April 1938.

ENGLAND—SOUTH AFRICA S

ENGLAND (Southampton)—EGYPT—ANGLO-EGYPTIAN SUDAN—BRITISH AND
AFRICA—UNION OF SOUTH AFRICA (Durban)   *Operated throughout*

SOUTH-BOUND

MILES from Southampton	PORTS OF CALL Junctions shown in CAPITALS *See notes at foot*	Local Standard Time	Day of Services Beginning Tuesday 12 April 1938			Local Standard Time	Day of Services Beginning Saturday 9 April 1938			
			Every Tues.	*Every* Thur.	*Every* Fri.		*Every* Tues.	*Every* Wed.	*Every* Thur.	*Every* Sat.
	LONDON (*Waterloo*) 🚌...............dep.	19 30	Tues.	Thur.	Fri.	19 30	Tues.	Wed.	Thur.	Sat.
	Southampton *England* .... 🚌 arr.	21 28	,,	,,	,,	21 28	,,	,,	,,	,,
	SOUTHAMPTON...............dep.	05 45	Wed.	Fri.	Sat.	05 15	Wed.	Thur.	Fri.	Sun.
422	Macon *France*.....................dep.	09 10	,,	,,	,,	Morn.	,,	,,	,,	,,
619	Marseilles *France*................dep.	11 00	,,	,,	,,	10 30	,,	,,	,,	,,
989	Rome *Italy* ....dep.	14 05	,,	,,	,,	13 35	,,	,,	,,	,,
1303	Brindisi *Italy*...................dep.	16 45	,,	,,	,,	16 15	,,	,,	,,	,,
1672	Athens *Greece* .... 🚌 arr.	Even.	,,	,,	,,	Even.	,,	,,	,,	,,
	Athens ....dep.	05 00	Thur.	Sat.	Sun.	06 00	Thur.	Fri.	Sat.	Mon
2259	ALEXANDRIA *Egypt* ....dep.	10 40	,,	,,	,,	Morn.	arr.	,,	,,	,,
2375	Cairo *Egypt* ....dep.	12 00	,,	,,	,,					
2693	Luxor *Egypt* ....dep.	14 35	,,	,,	,,					
2971	Wadi Halfa *Anglo-Egyptian Sudan* 🚌 arr.	Aftn.	,,	,,	,,					
	Wadi Halfa ....dep.	04 30	Fri.	Sun.	Mon.					
3415	KHARTOUM *Anglo-Egyptian Sudan* dep.	08 25	,,	,,	,,					
3840	Malakal *Anglo-Egyptian Sudan*.......dep.	11 55	,,	,,	,,					
4498	Port Bell (*Kampala*) *Uganda*..........dep.	18 20	,,	,,	,,					
4644	KISUMU *Kenya Colony*......... 🚌 arr.	Even.	,,	,,	,,					
	Kisumu ....dep.	06 30	Sat.		Tues.					
5080	Mombasa *Kenya Colony* ....dep.	10 35	,,		,,					
5273	Dar-es-Salaam *Tanganyika Territory*....dep.	12 25	,,		,,					
5494	Lindi *Tanganyika Territory*..........dep.	14 25	,,		,,					
5844	Mozambique *Port. E. Africa* 🚌 arr.	Aftn.	,,		,,					
	Mozambique.....................dep.	05 30	Sun.		Wed.					
6359	BEIRA *Port. E. Africa*............dep.	10 00	,,		,,					
6874	Lourenco Marques *Port. E. Africa*...dep.	14 50	,,		,,					
7161	DURBAN *Natal* ....arr.	Aftn.	,,		,,					

These services go on to
'Iraq, India, Burma,
Malaya, Hong Kong
and Australia

SOUTHAMPTON
NOTE. The Saturday service ex Southampton to Durban will leave at 05.15 and will operate 30 mins. earlier throughout the day to Athens

ALEXANDRIA
Junction for Imperial Airways service to and from India, Malaya, the Far East, Hong Kong and Australia

KHARTOUM
Junction for Imperial Airways Service to and from Nigeria (Lagos), and Elders Colonial Airways Service between Nigeria (Lagos) and Gold Coast (Accra) and vice versa

A call will be made at the following places if inducement offers and circumstances

PASSENGERS SPEND THE NIGHT AT
SOUTHAMPTON   South Western Hotel
MARSEILLES   Hotel de Noailles
ROME   Grande Hotel de Russie
BRINDISI   Hotel Internationale
ATHENS   Grande Bretagne
ALEXANDRIA   Hotel Cecil
WADI HALFA   Nile Hotel
KHARTOUM   Grand Hotel
KISUMU   Kisumu Hotel
MOZAMBIQUE   Rest House
By train between London and Southampton

PORTS OF CALL — Junctions shown in CAPITALS — *See notes at foot*	Local Standard Time	Day of Services Beginning Sunday 10 April, 1938		
		Every		*Every*
DURBAN *Natal* .... dep.	06 30	Sun.		Thur.
Lourenco Marques *P. E. Africa* dep.	09 15	,,		,,
BEIRA *Port. E. Africa* ...... dep.	13 55	,,		,,
Mozambique *Port. E. Africa* arr.	Even.	,,		,,
Mozambique .... dep.	06 00	Mon.		Fri.
Lindi *Tanganyika Territory* .... dep.	09 45	,,		,,
Dar-es-Salaam *Tanganyika Ter.* dep.	11 50	,,		,,
Mombasa *Kenya Colony* ...... dep.	13 35	,,		,,
KISUMU *Kenya Colony* arr.	Aftn.	,,	*Every*	,,
Kisumu .... dep.	07 00	Tues.	Fri.	Sat.
Port Bell (*Kampala*) *Uganda* .. dep.	08 30	,,	,,	,,
Malakal *Anglo-Egyptian Sudan* . dep.	13 25	,,	,,	,,
KHARTOUM *A-E Sudan* arr.	Aftn.	,,	,,	,,
Khartoum .... dep.	07 00	Wed.	Sat.	Sun.
Wadi Halfa *A-E Sudan* .... dep.	11 10	,,	,,	,,
Luxor *Egypt* .... dep.	13 40	,,	,,	,,
Cairo *Egypt* .... dep.	16 25	,,	,,	,,
Alexandria *Egypt* .... arr.	Aftn.	,,	,,	,,
ALEXANDRIA .... dep.	04 45	Thur.	Sun.	Mon.
Athens *Greece* .... dep.	10 05	,,	,,	,,
Brindisi *Italy* .... arr.	Morn.	,,	,,	,,
Brindisi .... dep.	12 20	,,	,,	,,
Rome *Italy* .... arr.	Aftn.	,,	,,	,,
Rome .... dep.	15 25	,,	,,	,,
Marseilles *France* .... arr.	Even.	,,	,,	,,
Marseilles .... dep.	06 15	Fri.	Mon.	Tues.
Macon *France* .... dep.	08 15	,,	,,	,,
Southampton *England* ...... arr.	Morn.	,,	,,	,,
LONDON (*Waterloo*) .... arr.	Aftn.	[train]	[train]	[train]

Before Wednesday, 20 April, there will be departures from Alexandria on Sat. 9 April, Mon. 11 April, Fri. 15 April, and Sun. 17 April, stopping the night at Brindisi and on Mon. 11 April, Thur. 14 April, Sun. 17 April, stopping the night at Rome

These services will operate to the same times as the new services shown below, and arrive in Southampton the following day, with the exception of that on Mon. 9 April, which also stops the night at St. Nazaire, arriving Southampton on 12 April.

These services have come from Australia, Malaya, Hong Kong, Burma, India and 'Iraq

Local Standard Time	Day of Services Beginning Wednesday 20 April, 1938		Local Standard Time	Day of Services Beginning Thursday 21 April, 1938	
	Every	*Every*		*Every*	*Every*
06 45	Wed.	Sat.	13 00	Thur.	Sun.
12 05	,,	,,	18 30	,,	,,
Aftn.	,,	,,	Even.	[boat]	[boat]
14 20	,,	,,	06 00	Fri.	Mon.
Aftn.	[boat]	[boat]	Morn.	,,	,,
07 00	Thur.	Sun.	09 05	,,	,,
Morn.	,,	,,	Morn.	,,	,,
10 15	,,	,,	12 20	,,	,,
12 15	,,	,,	14 20	,,	,,
Aftn.	,,	,,	Aftn.	,,	,,
Even.	[train]	[train]	Even.	[train]	[train]

KISUMU
Junction for Wilson Airways Services to Nairobi and Northern Rhodesia (Lusaka)

BEIRA
Junction for Rhodesian and Nyasaland Airways Services to Southern Rhodesia (Salisbury and Bulawayo) and Nyasaland (Blantyre)

DURBAN
Junction for South African Airways Services to Johannesburg

...LLA, KAREIMA, KOSTI, BUTIABA, QUELIMANE and INHAMBANE

to India, South Africa and Australia through the 1930s. While these 'red routes' were of symbolic importance, the practicalities were somewhat elaborate. Restrictions on overflying European countries meant that passengers were encouraged to undertake the Continental segment of their journey on the Venice Simplon-Orient-Express. The short flight duration of passenger planes meant that they had to make many stops for refuelling and overnighting. The fiction of the route being entirely over British territory was maintained by creating compounds at places such as Basra, where the alien surroundings were literally curtained off from passengers taking tea and rest in a canvas outpost of Britain.

That the stopping points on these 'Empire' routes were quite makeshift was less important than their cartographic coherence. Aviation literature and posters from the late 1920s and 1930s were full of maps. The Dutch KLM and the French Lignes Aériennes Farman and Lignes Aériennes Latécoère were all founded in 1919, Imperial Airways in 1924 and Lufthansa in 1926, all of whom worked to extend their small European countries' reach over the globe. Now that the 'conquest of the air' had been made, the aerial conquest of the world was left to play for. Germany had already had a hand in New World aviation through its financing of SCADTA (the Colombian–German Air Transport Society), the world's second passenger airline, which was founded in Colombia in 1919. In response to the prospect of German influence in Latin America and the Caribbean, the United States government subsidized the creation of Pan American Airways, which went on to dominate aviation in Latin America through the 1920s and 1930s. In Europe, Lufthansa flew more miles and carried more passengers than all the other European airlines combined; it also competed with Imperial Airways in Africa.

It was a race not only for passenger markets, but also for geographical trophies. The American Commander Richard Byrd made flights over the North and South Poles in the late 1920s. It was pique at these achievements that spurred on the team mounting the 1933 British flight over Mount Everest, which was financed by Lucy, Lady Houston. The race to the summit of the mountain had defeated Britain's best climbers, George Mallory and Andrew Irvine, who had disappeared there six years earlier; instead this expedition sought scopic dominance. As an intertitle from the resulting film announced: 'For the first time, man was to look down on the roof of the world.' The visual record and publicity element of the expedition was there from the outset, with the inclusion of cameramen in the team and the decision to use two planes (one to film from). In 1934 the aerial views

of Everest were shown to cinema-goers, with the team of pilots and crew portrayed as classically nonchalant; the film even won an Oscar. It is worth noting that this great achievement was made possible only by funding from Charles Grey, a figure closely allied with fascism. Indeed, many of the most prominent figures in the world of 1930s aviation were sympathetic to the Nazi cause, partly because German state funding of flying was so generous compared to the British government's meagre subsidies. Grey wrote openly racist and anti-Semitic editorials throughout his long career as editor of the *Aeroplane* magazine.

Cinema, print journalism (especially illustrated journals) and radio put aviation before the public in ever more ways from the early 1930s, with races, expeditions and new designs generating news. Imperial Airways funded a series of short and long documentaries about civil aviation in the Empire. This was both promotional and conceived as a public education programme. The airline also commissioned the design of a symbol, the Speedbird, that over the 1930s would feature on merchandise, on increasingly stylized posters, and in the dynamic and colourful advertising short by Len Lye, 'Colour Flight' (1938). Croydon Airport was the subject of the BBC's *Children's Hour* programme in 1934, and in the same year the ex-pilot and experimental broadcaster Lance Sieveking's programme *Airways of Empire* was broadcast as part of the BBC National Programme, offering 'A panorama in sound representing the development of flying from the Middle Ages up to this Moment'.[47] The Soviet Union went one step further in using the aeroplane as a propaganda tool, with the construction of the gigantic Tupolev Maxim Gorki. As well as being the world's largest ever aeroplane, catering for seventy passengers, the Maxim Gorki carried a printing press, a 'Voice

ABOVE: Imperial Airways Short Empire flying boat, on the cover of the first flying number of *The Bystander*, 3 May 1939. OPPOSITE: View from *The Pilots' Book of Everest* by Sir D. Douglas-Hamilton and Lieut. D. F. Macintyre, 1936. PAGE 159: Commander Richard E. Byrd flying over the North Pole in a Fokker Trimotor monoplane. Illustration by Manning de V. Lee in *Historic Airships* by R. Holland, 1928.

ABOVE: Cancelled Soviet stamp showing the Tupolev Maxim Gorki, 1937.
OPPOSITE: A page of airmail stamps published in *L'Illustration*, 1932. OVERLEAF: The
airmail arriving in Rio de Janeiro, artwork from *L'Illustration*, 1932.

from the Sky' radio station and loudspeakers, a photography lab and a film
projector for showing films during flights or to audiences of thousands on
the ground. It was an audacious feat of design, but it lacked agility. In May
1935 it crashed into a much smaller biplane engaged in looping the loop
around it during a formation flying display over Moscow.

It was not only passenger aviation that saw assiduous promotion in the
1930s, but airmail too. The airline that attracted most popular interest on this
count was Pierre-Georges Latécoère's Lignes Aériennes. The businessman
and aeroplane manufacturer had decided early on to launch a mail service
between his base in Toulouse and the southern cone of Latin America.
All the points on this route were difficult to fly or to negotiate: over the
Pyrenees to Barcelona, down the coast of Spain, across to Morocco and
then west and south along the African coastline before the Atlantic crossing
between Dakar in Senegal and Natal in Brazil, and the arduous traverse of
the Andes to Santiago de Chile. Furthermore, Latécoère was determined
that planes should take off in any weather and fly through the night. For
this reason Aéropostale, as it later became known, convened a brotherhood
of the most intrepid French pilots that became famous for its bravery and
endurance, in an echo of the wartime aces. The company was mythologized
by several writers caught up in the romance of lives being risked for the sake
of the reputation of 'La Ligne', and by extension France itself. Among the
best known of these pilots was Jean Mermoz, a prominent Croix-de-Feu
member, and Antoine de Saint-Exupéry, who published *Southern Mail* and

Night Flight in 1929–31, followed by *Wind, Sand and Stars* in 1939. Saint-Exupéry's most famous book, *The Little Prince* (1943), was based on his own experience after an air crash in the Sahara desert.

Saint-Exupéry's novels were soon translated into a number of languages 165 and continue to capture the imagination with their vivid accounts of the transcendental experience of lone flying. Indeed, although Aéropostale was unique in its approach to risk, losing many more pilots than other airlines, there were plenty of other claims to adventure in this period. Long-distance challenges continued to be set and tried. Women came into their own as pilots, although they were still not employed to work commercially. Hélène Boucher's Paris–Saigon flight of 1929, Amy Johnson's solo England–Australia flight in 1930, Amelia Earhart's solo Atlantic crossing in 1932 and Jean Batten's solo England–Australia and England–New Zealand flights in 1934 and 1936 gave female aviators greater visibility and credibility. Affordable light flying craft such as the De Havilland Moth enabled those of lesser means to try their hand at flight; many of the above milestones were completed in Moths which were popular for leisure flying, since, with their wings folded, they fitted in a garage.

The call for air-mindedness that had been made by aviation proponents in the 1920s was renewed in the early 1930s, with initiatives in most countries aimed at boys and young men. In Germany the Air Sports Association, created in 1933, took over all existing flying clubs and societies, including the very popular gliding groups, making the activity a central one for Hitler Youth members. In the United States the Rockefeller brothers financed the Air Youth of America. In Britain the Air Defence Cadet Corps was set up in 1938 and the Air Scouts in 1941. Aviation figured largely in debates over rearmament, as the flying community in Britain, which had long bemoaned the lack of government investment, grew justifiably anxious at Germany's enthusiastic transformation of its civil flying activities into military ones. Among the many aviation questions raised in the House of Commons in the 1930s was that of female pilots: was it a waste of money to subsidize women's flying lessons if they were not permitted to fly in a war?

Though there was a clear affinity between nationalist parties and aviation, many European liberal thinkers and politicians leaned strongly towards bringing both civil and military aviation under the control of an international power. It was suggested in the late 1920s by Winston Churchill among others that the League of Nations could maintain world peace if France, Britain and the United States could submit their air power to

ABOVE: Jean Batten after her arrival in Sydney. From her book *My Life*, 1938.
OPPOSITE: The De Havilland Hornet Moth, in flight and in the garage.
Advertisement in *The Aeroplane*, 31 July 1935.

its control. André Tardieu, the French minister of war, was particularly keen on this idea as it would have given France, which had the smallest air force, greater protection against Germany. The British Labour Party thought international control would also do away with wasteful market competition. Fears about how the British Empire would be controlled without a British air force were addressed by the suggestion that superannuated biplanes be retained, 'obsolete in a modern war, but good enough for policing semi-civilized tribes'.[48] The idea was opposed not only by the fascist members of the League of Nations, who exited the association one by one through the 1930s, but also by the representatives of manufacturers, who saw no advantage for business.

There was a tremendous appetite for flight stories between the wars. Juveniles continued to sell well, but the most exciting and colourful periodicals came from the United States. In reaction to these stories, which he claimed distorted and even usurped the feats of British pilots, Flying Officer William Earl Johns began writing. Johns had begun his journalism career in aviation art, putting his RFC expertise to use in illustrating material

HORNET
MOTH

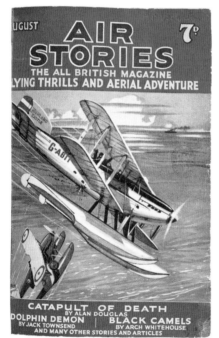

ABOVE: Covers of *Air Stories*: July, June, August and December 1935.
OPPOSITE: Cover of *The Modern Boy*, 7 January 1933.

The MODERN BOY

EVERY SATURDAY.

Week Ending January 7th, 1933.

No. 257.

Vol. 10.

2D.

WAR-TIME FLYING STORY, by FLYING-OFFICER JOHNS, *Inside!*

POPULAR FLYING

6^D

AUGUST 1932

F-AIXV

ABOVE: Covers of *Biggles Learns to Fly!* (1935) and *Biggles: Pioneer Air Fighter* (1954).
OPPOSITE: Cover of *Popular Flying*, August 1932.

for Hendon aerial pageants and covers for *Air* magazine. He was a contributor alongside Alan Cobham to *The Modern Boy*, an aviation-centred weekly magazine launched in 1928, and was made editor of a new title, *Popular Flying*, in 1932. This non-specialist aviation monthly was an immediate success and sold 30,000 copies a month through the decade. It was a mixture of 'Thrilling Flight' accounts, mainly by war veterans, and commentary by contemporary civil aviators, including women, all held together by Johns's rambling but entertaining notes 'From the Editor's Cockpit'. It was here that the Biggles stories first appeared. Johns went on to write over a hundred Biggles novels until his death in 1968. He was fired from his editorship in the late 1930s after his continual criticism of the government's slowness to train pilots and set up air defence bases, but he made a significant contribution to the recruitment and morale of generations of RAF personnel.

The particular appeal of Johns's drawings lay in their combination of attractive colours and composition with accurate detailing. The variety of makes and models of aircraft, along with easily accessible airfields, encouraged hobbyist taxonomies, with plane spotters and collectors of imagery maintaining a keen interest in new airframe production. Publishers and businesses saw an opportunity in the 1930s to reflect and encourage this trend. For example, *Popular Flying* ran visual puzzles inviting readers to cut out and rearrange a collection of drawings of flying aeroplanes into a dogfight. In 1932 Skybirds model aeroplane kits went on sale. Made of

ABOVE: Skybird club no. 152 (Motherwell) with 84 scale models they had assembled and painted. From *The Skybird*, 1934. OPPOSITE, TOP: Advertisement for model aeroplanes available at Hamleys, from *Popular Flying*, 1932. OPPOSITE, BOTTOM: Cover of *Skybirds: Descriptive Details* by J. H. Stevens, 1935.

wood with some metal elements, the kits were marketed at those aged 12 and over. The company encouraged the foundation of local model-making clubs, which together formed the Skybird League – a community with its own quarterly magazine, whose aircraft could enter competitions and end up being displayed in the windows of the London toyshop Hamleys.

Skybirds kits were explicitly designed to tutor their assemblers in the fine details of aircraft construction, and were approved by educational and air-minded organizations. A feature often remarked on was the way in which models enabled makers to play with scale and photography: 'If a Skybirds model is constructed properly, it should be hard to distinguish a photograph of it from one of an actual machine of the same type.'[49] Modellers could compete with expensive air-to-air photography by making a record of their aircraft suspended in 'flight' or nestled in a diorama of airport accessories. They could participate in the drama of an air show or a dogfight in a new way. Readers of the *Skybird* sent in their photographs, hoping that they would be good enough for publication. 'My aerodrome is laid out on my bedroom floor', wrote one boy who had put together twenty-four model aeroplanes and enjoyed enacting air pageants with them. Another observed: 'The craze has spread like wildfire at school and in my district at home, it beats Yo-Yo and Bif Bat, etc., hollow [...] We are all air-minded.'[50]

8   'Beware Down Below'

> Oh earth, open thyself to receive us! For it is the
> moment when the stars are going to fall, or lacking
> this, something even more explosive and stinging!
> Beware down below!
> – Paul Claudel (1936)[51]

The romance of aviation, which in the 1930s was balanced between the evocation of wartime heroism and the construction of a strong and forward-looking national community of fliers, was tempered by the destruction of life and property that aeroplanes were eventually able to wreak. Since 1909 there had been many predictions that powered flight would transform warfare. The latest theorist of bombing was Giulio Douhet, an Italian writer in the 1920s, whose work was translated into English in the early 1930s.

Experiments in air policing had been going on since the end of the First World War. RAF control of 'rebel tribes' in Iraq and Sudan through bombing and strafing had been celebrated in the British press in the early 1920s. Aeroplanes played an important part in the brutal Italian subjugation of Cyreneica in Libya in the 1920s and early 1930s. In the Sino-Japanese war Japan had conducted several bombing campaigns over Chinese cities, and the results were disseminated in the international press. Aeroplanes extended the battleground in a war, and cities, with their civilian populations, became possible targets. The horrific potential of this was vividly realized in 1937, as the Spanish Civil War and the Second Sino-Japanese War raged. In November 1936 the Spanish air force, controlled by Franco's Nationalists, bombed Madrid, killing 133 civilians. In August 1937 the Shanghai International Settlement was attacked by Kuomintang bombers and over 3,000 Japanese civilians were killed.

It was the attack on Guernika, executed by the Condor Legion which Hitler had mustered from requisitioned Lufthansa planes to help

DESERT WARRIOR
The sharp-toothed charger of this RAF pilot, photographed in the Libyan desert, is a Curtiss "Kittyhawk."

Franco transport troops, that really changed perceptions of aerial bombing in Europe. Responsibility was initially denied by the Luftwaffe, but this offensive in April 1937, aimed at cutting off the northward retreat of Basque Republican troops, was evidently a German experiment in air power involving extensive bombardment and strafing. The attack lasted several hours, killing up to 1,600 and destroying 70 per cent of the town centre. The emblematic memorial by Pablo Picasso, painted and displayed in controversial circumstances at the 1937 International Exhibition in Paris, extended the agony and uncertainty suffered by the town's inhabitants into a diffuse, generalized terror that civilians the world over would begin to experience as war became inevitable. 'Everytown' was the name chosen for the site of a devastating bomb attack in the 1936 Alexander Korda film *Things to Come*, based, of course, on an H. G. Wells novel. In 1938 psychologists convened as part of a panel to assess the potential impact of aerial attack in Britain predicted that the number of civilians mentally affected by bombs would be three or four times greater than that of those physically affected, and contingency plans for an exodus of up to 4 million people from the capital were discussed.

The outbreak of the Second World War in 1939 would put to the test the military aviation materiel and policies developed in Europe over the preceding decade. The interwar obsession with gliding, the canny focus of resources on its civilian airline Lufthansa, and the Nazis' contravention of international sanctions in reviving the Luftwaffe in the second half of the 1930s meant that Germany was well resourced to conduct the bulk of its territorial expansion with air power, or *Blitzkrieg*. As well as repurposing the airliners into long-distance bomber planes, the Luftwaffe had a new dive bomber, the Junkers Ju 87, or Stuka, and an impressive fighter plane, the Messerschmitt Bf 109. The RAF was the only national air force in opposition to Hitler until the United States joined the war in 1941. It was smaller (as was Britain's army) and, while the Fleet Air Arm was the largest of any navy, its machines were outdated. But, unlike Germany, Britain had invested in a strategic bombing plan, including the development of heavy bomber planes, and in a civil defence system using radar and operations rooms to detect aerial attacks on the island and to strategize and track the RAF response.

ABOVE: Front cover of number 3 in the Puffin Picture Book series on the RAF, *War in the Air*, by James Gardner, 1940. OPPOSITE: The Supermarine Spitfire Mark V, the Curtis Kittyhawke and a group of fighter pilots, on pages from *Flying and Popular Aviation*, September 1942. PAGE 174: Poster made by the Spanish Ministry of Propaganda, 1936–39.

ANTI-AIRCRAFT SOUND LOCATOR

GLOUCESTER GAUNTLET
INTERCEPTOR FIGHTERS

REPRESENTATION OF BALLOON
BARRAGE FOR DEFENCE OF LONDON

REPRESENTATION OF AIR DEFENCE CONTROL ROOM

PILOTS RUNNING TO MACHINES
TO TAKE OFF

ANTI-AIRCRAFT SEARCHLIGHT

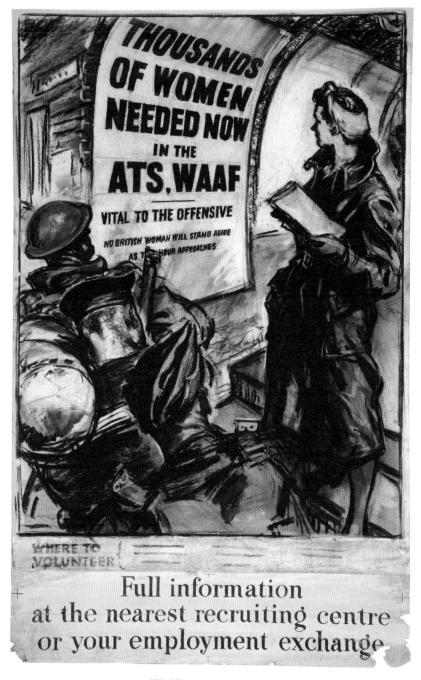

ABOVE: WAAF recruitment poster, 1939–45.
OPPOSITE: Wills cigarette cards 'Air Raid Precautions' series, 1938.

While the accoutrements of aerial defence and attack (searchlights, anti-aircraft guns, barrage balloons, deft fighter pilots with agile machines) would have been familiar from the previous war, the complexion of the British air force was slightly different this time around. Its higher echelons were still occupied by white upper-class men, but they were joined by a far more cosmopolitan range of airmen and engineers from the Commonwealth and occupied Europe. Squadrons of Polish and Czech pilots, activated as a last resort during the Battle of Britain, were a significant help. The ground crews, who made up the bulk of the force and were indispensable to the work of the pilots, still suffered from a lack of prestige in the rigid social hierarchy that prevailed in the RAF, as well as a lack of recognition after the war. There was a greater drive to recruit women to the Women's Auxiliary Air Force (WAAF), which was founded at the outbreak of war and was 180,000 strong by 1943. William Johns was asked by the Air Ministry to turn his pen to a female air heroine and Joan 'Worrals' Worralson came into being, for a run of eleven novels that outlasted the war. The Aerial Transport Auxiliary, after pressure from the well-connected British pilot Pauline Gower, allowed female pilots to transport aircraft and personnel, and the novelty of this corps of women was exploited by press photographers. WAAFs did a great deal of the computing and communications behind

ABOVE: WAAF member operating a barrage balloon winch. From *Flying and Popular Aviation*, September 1942. OPPOSITE: Female Aerial Transport Auxiliary (ATA) pilots, from *Flying and Popular Aviation*, September 1942.

aerial operations, from interpreting aerial photographs and operating radios and telephones to plotting the movement of squadrons in the operations room. The manning of barrage balloons, a physically gruelling and cumbersome task, was detailed to WAAF squadrons. They were paid two-thirds as much as their male equivalents.

The Soviet Union was the only state that allowed women to fly in combat, giving them special responsibilities for stealth bombing. Their 588th Night Bomber Regiment flew in small, slow biplanes with open cockpits, switching off their engines before gliding over the target and releasing their payload. The quiet rush of their planes' wings earned them the nickname of 'Night Witches' from the Germans.

Just as the blackout had effected a new-found siege mentality in the cities under bombardment in 1915–18, the air-raid precautions imposed in Britain were formative in the wartime atmosphere. Gas masks, mass evacuation, air-raid shelters both purpose-built and improvised, the wail of the warning siren, the ethos of 'keep calm and carry on' – these associations, arising from the threat of aerial attack on British cities, are still ingrained in our national memory. The threats were anticipated, with rhetoric about

'knock-out blows' leading planners to overestimate the extent of potential damage in the years leading up to war. In fact both German and British air forces were ready to begin bombing civilian targets, but neither wanted to be the first to attack and to trigger retaliation. In September 1939 the Luftwaffe carpet-bombed Warsaw. A celebratory film about the bombing, *Feuertaufe*, was screened in Germany. The bombing killed 30,000 people, most of them civilians, and wiped out the city centre. A year later, after successful German bombardments of Rotterdam and Paris, British commanders initiated attacks on Germany and dispatched bombing missions to the industrial Ruhr Valley.

The Battle of Britain, which took place in July and August 1940, has had far more historical prominence in post-victory narratives than the British bombing campaigns. It presents a more favourable story, sketching national attributes large in the sky like the flurry of contrails recorded in Paul Nash's famous painting *The Battle of Britain* (1941). The Supermarine Spitfire, which alongside the De Havilland Mosquito was used to fight off a far greater number of German bombers and fighters invading British airspace, became symbolic of British engineering and design. In fact the RAF was pushed to breaking point, with hundreds of pilots killed, many of them not by enemy action but by technical malfunction or their inexpert handling of the aeroplanes. Though the Germans were prevented by British

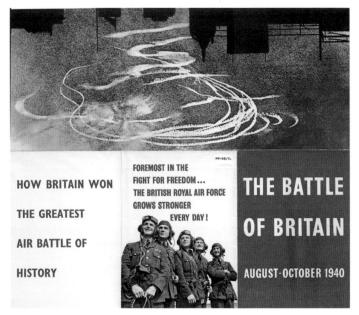

TOP: Cover of Puffin book *The Battle of Britain* by D. Garnett and J. Gardner, c.1941.
BOTTOM: 'The Battle of Britain', Ministry of Information propaganda leaflet, c.1940–1.
OPPOSITE: Yevdokia Bershanskaya, commander of the 46th Guards Night Bomber
Regiment (formerly the 588th Night Bomber Regiment), instructs Yevdokia Nosal and
Nina Ulyanenko, 1942.

184

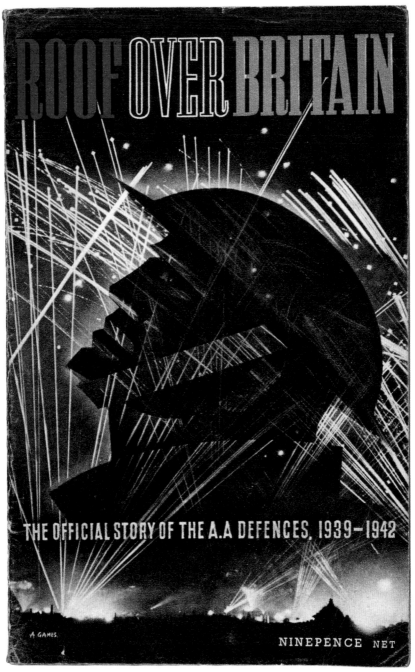

'Roof over Britain', Ministry of Information propaganda book, 1945.

'The Proud City', London Transport poster designed by W. E. Spradbery, 1944.

air superiority from invading Britain, they were able to continue bombing London and other industrially important cities with some success.

For all its undeniable horror and suffering, the Blitz provided Londoners with a daily spectacle comparable to the ghoulish expectations of thousands of Victorians who crowded into pleasure gardens to watch a balloon ascent that might end in a dramatic disaster. From the first attacks, some Londoners were described by onlookers as relishing the risks, cheering from the stands of football matches or greyhound races as bombs fell shy of them or planes were shot down. The raids were often described as beautiful, and those lucky enough not to be in the target areas would gather at balconies to watch the gala of *son et lumieres*. Al Alvarez described it:

> air-raid sirens wailing, the steady rise and fall of the bomber engines (the radio newsreaders talked about 'waves of bombers', and that was how they sounded), bombs whistling ... the thump of anti-aircraft batteries on Primrose Hill, planes pinned against the night sky in a latticework of searchlights, the eerie glow over London the night the City caught fire.[52]

It reached the point where the Ministry of Information felt the need to issue a poster with the instructions 'In a raid – Don't stand and stare at the sky. Take cover at once'.

The aftermath of the destruction also exerted fascination. Rebecca West visited London the day after a raid and 'made myself dizzy by swivelling round to look out of the back window [of a taxi] to see, against the blue sky, the trails of exhaust fumes which marked a fight between a German and an English plane'.[53] Children would scamper over bombsites looking for spoils, revelling in these newly created adventure playgrounds. Blitz tourists would travel into London on a Sunday to spectate the smouldering wreckage of a raid.

The former French ambassador to the United States, Paul Claudel, had suggested in 1936 that the best air-raid warning came from the biblical book of Revelation, with its premonitions of destruction from above. The aerial bombing that took place later in the Second World War showed the anxieties of 1930s civil society to have been well founded. Forty thousand British civilians were killed by the Luftwaffe, but ten times more Germans died in the joint British and American strikes on German cities in 1943–5.

R.A.F. day raiders over Berlin's official quarter.

THE DOWNFALL OF THE DICTATORS IS ASSURED

PRINTED FOR H.M. STATIONERY OFFICE BY FOSH & CROSS LTD., LONDON. 51-3961

ABOVE: 'Bomber Command', Ministry of Information propaganda leaflet,
1939–45. PREVIOUS PAGE: 'The Downfall of the Dictators is Assured', Ministry
of Information propaganda poster, 1939–45.

The Allied raids, planned some years before the war, were designed for
maximum impact and often killed tens of thousands. The death toll could
reach 37,000 in one night, as in Hamburg in July 1943, when a firestorm
developed during bombardment. The destruction of Hamburg, Dresden,
Munich and other German cities was absolutely devastating to the population as a whole, and the reputation of the British Bomber Command,
which carried out these attacks, has never recovered. It was at this stage of
catastrophic civilian losses that a new form of weapon was unveiled, the
German 'vengeance' missiles V-1 and V-2.

Each day V-1 cruise missiles were launched at south-east England
from occupied French bases over the summer of 1944. They would whistle
ominously as they shot into the midst of the capital at speeds faster than
British fighter planes, to kill dozens on detonation. Though ways were
found, with difficulty, to divert or destroy these 'doodlebugs', they wreaked
significant psychological damage. Only weeks after the French bases had
been overpowered and disarmed, V-2 guided ballistic missiles were ready
for deployment from mobile launchers in northern Europe. These had been
developed from the 1930s by scientists influenced by the American Robert

Goddard's experiments with liquid-propulsion rockets. A German V-2 test rocket was the first man-made object to reach outer space, and at the war's end the Americans and the Soviets made haste to grab their share of V-2 expertise and facilities, which would form the nuclei of their respective space programmes. The uncanny supersonic speed of the rockets, confounding radars, anti-aircraft guns and aerial pursuit, and their capacity for killing hundreds on impact, acted with even greater effect on British morale. But the crowning air atrocity of the Second World War was the use of another hastily reached milestone of twentieth-century science, the atomic bomb, on the cities of Hiroshima and Nagasaki in 1945. With their death tolls of hundreds of thousands and their enduring effects on the health of the populations, these weapons heralded a new level of total war that remains (in theory) in place today. Richard Overy points out that these attacks were the culmination of a five-year strategic bombing campaign by the British and American air forces, finally constituting the much anticipated 'knock-out blow'.[54]

The airborne weaponry developed during the Second World War laid the ground for the rival forms of geopolitical leverage exercised during the Cold War that followed. The seventeenth-century Jesuit Lana di Terzi had suggested that the achievement of flight would disturb the civil and political balance of mankind. With the termination of the Second World War, it was very evident that flight had enabled humans to rain destruction upon one another. But if humankind had become 'Shiva, the destroyer of worlds' (as the American nuclear physicist J. Robert Oppenheimer quoted from the *Bhagavad Gita* decades later), it had also found a way of exploring new worlds outside the earth's atmosphere, another long-held ambition associated with flight. The nuclear threat and the space race were parallel concerns that would loom large in popular culture around the world through the 1950s and 1960s.

All through the conflict, fears and tensions were played out by children with toy aeroplanes. Besides Skybirds models, ready-made miniatures had gone into production in the 1930s, as Meccano, which had been manufacturing tin-plate construction toys and vehicles for several decades, began making die-cast aeroplanes alongside cars at its Liverpool factory. Together with printed imagery such as cardboard games, cigarette cards, stamps and the pages of magazines such as *Popular Flying*, miniature aircraft enabled children to engage from a young age with aircraft and their social, cultural and national meanings. Although toy production slowed significantly

WOMEN MUST WORK

Women employees working in a Westland Aircraft factory

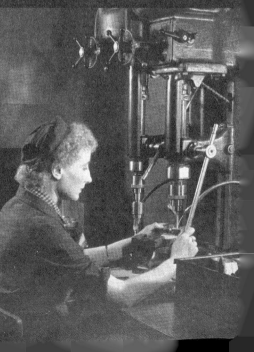

during the war (the Germans were the world's leading toy manufacturers, and most British toy factories were used for war work), a special edition model Spitfire was being sold in order to raise funds to make more of the real thing. It is a sign of the entrenched appeal of the aeroplane to children that, during the war, model Spitfires were made from anything they, or their loving parents, could lay their hands on.

Comics, which had begun to replace the *fin de siècle* format of the juveniles, also played an important part in the imagination of 1940s children. In the United States newly invented superhero characters such as Superman, Captain Marvel and Batman were all airborne by the end of the war. It was actually five years after Superman first appeared in DC comics (in 1933) that he was given the power of flight; by contrast Batman, a character commissioned in 1939 in the wake of Superman's success, was conceived by Bob Kane with a bat-wing carapace inspired by Leonardo da Vinci's ornithopter, pictures of which he had seen as a child. In Britain, which began to see a trickle of these American comics only in the 1950s, when they arrived as ship ballast, adventure trumped superhuman powers. Dan Dare was the British response to Cold War heroics, a Biggles-type figure who reiterated narratives of imperial expansion and defence in outer space just as the nation's empire on earth was falling away.

Despite the once unprecedented scale of destruction and death that aeroplanes had been seen to wreak, the post-war legacy of aviation was more complex than it had been in 1918. Wartime aircraft manufacture had generated widespread employment. The networks of domestic and international civil aviation were already established. Air power had won the war, and it was likely that future national security lay in the air. As the dust settled on new geopolitical arrangements in Europe and the Far East, Allied air force partners could prove their continued utility by taking supplies to the city of Berlin, blockaded on the ground by Stalin's Soviet forces in 1948–9. One enterprising American pilot was very fondly remembered as 'Uncle Wiggle-Wings' or 'The Chocolate Bomber' after scattering the city with sweets as he went about his duties.

OPPOSITE: 'Women Must Work': female employees working in a Westland Aircraft factory, from *Aeronautics*, August 1941. OVERLEAF: A group of German children cheering a United States cargo plane as it flies over a western section of Berlin, 1948–49.

HARPER'S

Bazaar

British
Flight
of
Fashion

April 1956

Three Shillings and Sixpence

The Jet Age

Fly me to the moon, and let me play among the
stars; Let me see what spring is like on Jupiter
and Mars.
– Bart Howard, 'In other Words' (1954)[55]

The year 1952 was a rare one for British aviation – one of triumph on the
world stage. With the De Havilland Comet, British aeronautics won the
race to produce a jet airliner using the technology invented by RAF engineer
Frank Whittle. American and Soviet engineers were also working hard to
implement the jet-powered aircraft that would go on to loom large in the
Cold War, but for a few moments it was British design and manufacture
that dominated. In contrast to the period following the First World War,
the late 1940s and early 1950s saw aviation companies well supported by the
government, with air power having proven its worth most decisively, and
British expertise playing an important part in the close dependence Britain
now had on the United States.

The cultural presence of flight was also strong. For all the war casualties,
of personnel and of civilians, aviation now exerted a powerful pull on the
popular imagination, drawing on a mixture of Blitz-forged resilience, the
prevailing plucky underdog narrative of the Battle of Britain and confidence in a new jet-powered future. Something similar had happened in
the period 1919–22, with new aviation routes across the globe and veteran
aces rehabilitated as imperial connectors. Now ex-fighter pilots became test
pilots for aircraft manufacturers. Badly paid and facing an incredibly low life
expectancy, they were possibly the most admired men in the country. 'They
are the New Elizabethans,' declared the *Daily Express*: 'By their courage,
they have given Britain the chance to become mistress of the skies.'

ABOVE: Advertisement for Airspeed Ambassador high-speed airliner, on the cover of *Flight and Aircraft Engineer*, 6 March 1947. PAGE 194: 'The British Flight of Fashion.' Cover of *Harper's Bazaar*, April 1956.

Once again boundaries of nature were conjured up to replace enemy aircraft, with the sound barrier working as a compelling adversary for both pilots and engineers. *The Sound Barrier* (1952), David Lean's well-received film on the subject, which ignored the fact that the American pilot Chuck Yeager had already achieved Mach 1, presented a convincing British tale of ambitious manufacturers, test pilots dutiful enough to die for the cause and the sympathetic voice of reason being drowned out by the awesomeness of the sonic boom. Churchill loved the film and, despite its gentle hints at hubris and its foregrounding of death, it helped to promote both military and commercial flying. The combination of extreme risk and potential glory also drew hundreds of thousands to air shows, now run by a consortium of manufacturers rather than by the RAF, where famous test pilots took prototype aircraft to their operational limits in order to impress both potential buyers and the crowds. These were legendary events as much for their disasters as for their smooth running. At Farnborough in September 1952 John Derry crashed after performing a supersonic dive in the De Havilland DH. 110, killing himself, his assistant and twenty-nine spectators. That Derry's friend Neville Duke went on to perform another dive and sonic

boom in a Hawker Hunter that afternoon testifies to the very different
approach to grief left over from the war: not only did the ex-RAF service-
men carry on with their work undeterred by the closeness of death, but it
was deemed appropriate to continue an event with the blood of dozens
of audience members freshly spilt on Observation Hill. Far from being
deterred by the risk to life for all involved, another 20,000 people turned
up to the show the next day, making 140,000 in total.

197

As well as showing off the Supermarine Swift, which served as the
supersonic 'Prometheus' in the film, and the De Havilland Vampire, in
which the leading couple fly from Hatfield to Cairo for lunch, *The Sound
Barrier* offered the Comet a very attractive cameo. This was the pride of the
British Overseas Airways Corporation (BOAC), the airline constituted by
the nationalization and merger of IA and BA in 1940 (also forming British
European Airways). BOAC Comets carried thirty-six passengers in first class,
and in smooth silence compared to the noisy cabins of propeller-driven
planes. If the Comet was a big step up from predecessors such as the iconic
Short Empire flying boats that had been used for long-distance travel in
the 1940s, it was light years from W. S. Henson's Arial, nicknamed the
Comet, advertised 109 years earlier. But its imagery shared something with
the Victorian steam plane. Just as the Arial's publicist had commissioned

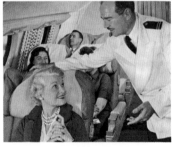

ABOVE LEFT: Advertisement for BOAC (1960), featuring an attendant looking after
an elderly passenger: 'Their confidence is catching.' ABOVE RIGHT: Cover of
Wings over the World, BOAC magazine, May 1946.

One side of a folded leaflet/poster advertising the
BOAC Comet 4 Jetliner, 1956.

views of it over the Pyramids, its cutting-edge technology overlaid on an exotic landscape, so the Comet flew the imperial route over Africa in 1952. On its first scheduled flight it was seen off by thousands at Croydon and greeted by 20,000 in Johannesburg. A Pathé newsreel cameraman recorded the flight, dwelling on the juxtaposition of Britain's latest vehicle of progress with the natural wonders (and native wonder) of the African continent. A BBC documentary, *Comet over Africa* (1952), repeated these tropes for television audiences.

The elite nature of its payload only added to its appeal, with the rich and glamorous passengers disembarking the plane as much of a draw as the sleek, gleaming lines of the aircraft itself, both for spectators and for press photographers. In the early 1950s BOAC's Comets carried the new Queen Elizabeth, Princess Margaret and the Queen Mother, as well as the glamorous cousins of Geoffrey de Havilland, Olivia de Havilland and Joan Fontaine. With the jet age came the jet set, 'people who live fast and move fast', according to the American society journalist who coined the phrase.[56] This latest iteration of celebrity culture was explicitly linked to the new technological turn of flight. World leaders and dignitaries travelled by jet to perform their international duties, as did actors. The comical stage-managed emergence of the starlet Anita Ekberg from a Vickers Viscount turbojet in Federico Fellini's *La Dolce Vita* (1960) provided a visual template for the glamour of international aviation. It was now the passengers who were famous rather than the pilots. Shots of actors and musicians ascending or descending airliner steps proliferated in the press. British European Airways (BEA) placed its name strategically close to the door in order to benefit from the exposure. This worked particularly well when the Beatles travelled by BEA.

Part of the optimism about the jet age in Britain was based on the idea that high-end travel would boost the economy by providing good jobs. The aircraft industry had expanded massively during the war, and generous government spending on research and development kept the 'big six' companies (Bristol, De Havilland, English Electric, Hawker Siddeley, Rolls-Royce and Vickers Armstrong) big. Employment increased by 100,000 between 1950 and 1954, and remained above 279,000 until 1963. Eleven per cent of British engineers and scientists worked in the aircraft industry. As David Edgerton has pointed out, aircraft workers tended to be both happier about their products than their counterparts in car manufacturing and less likely to travel in them.[57] Aeroplanes were seen as a strong part of Britain's post-war economic identity, even after it was knocked off

ABOVE: Advertisement for the TWA Intercontinental Boeing 707, October 1959: 'So let yourself go and enjoy this great Jet Age Adventure.' OPPOSITE: The royal family at London Airport on 21 February 1957, from *British European Airways Magazine*.

its high horse of 1952. In the spring of 1954, after four total losses and many fatalities, it became clear that the first Comet was not a viable airliner for frequent flying. Within months the American firm Boeing had trialled the prototype of its 707 jet. By the time the Comet was modified for safe service in 1958, the Boeing 707 had taken its place as the world's leading jet airliner.

In the decade that followed, world passenger numbers increased sixfold. Despite the relatively small number of privileged passengers who took foreign holidays or flew for business in the 1960s, flight was being reconceptualized as an aspirational part of modern life. Flying took place visibly, regularly and relatively safely. In the United States, where aeroplanes offered a great speed advantage over terrestrial transport, domestic aviation had already become normalized. For Britain, it was the drive to southern sunshine that powered mass civil aviation. BEA began offering flights to Valencia and Lisbon, which at around £54 (£1,230 in today's money) were prohibitively expensive. Charter flights were integrated into packaged foreign holidays as early as 1950, though it was not until 1974 that they were allowed to undercut prices for scheduled airline services. It would take a further jet revolution to make commercial flying an affordable activity, with

ABOVE: 'BEA Silver Wing Holidays '66 Style'. Map and inside pages from a 1960s
BEA advertising brochure. OVERLEAF: Airfix advertisement, c.1959.

jumbo jets such as the Boeing 747 increasing passenger loads and reducing costs and fares from 1969.

If jet planes were still far from most people's reach, there was now an abundant supply of miniatures. After the war, entrepreneurs had been quick to make use of new-found plastics and injection-moulding technology to produce cheap and light model-making kits. Airfix had started out making combs and lighters and, after some years producing model ships, it hit upon the aeroplane, starting with the Spitfire in 1953. The kits were sold for 2 shillings at Woolworths, which put them within reach of children with pocket money, and soon became very popular. Airfix's profits grew by a factor of ten over the 1950s. They catered to a public that was passionate about details, having been tutored in aircraft spotting by wartime experience. Both the wartime and the latest models of aircraft were reproduced with reference to manufacturers' blueprints. Cheaper and therefore more expendable than the pre-war Skybirds models, they could be crashed and burned with some impunity. Arthur Ward remembers rushing out to get his first Airfix kit aged 5:

> With any luck I would have my newly purchased Spitfire – or Lancaster if it was my birthday – assembled by teatime, in time for bombing raids against an imaginary industrial complex hidden in the shrubbery. I'd probably have set my new replica alight before I bought the next Airfix kit. But as this represented direct hits by 'Hun' Flak it was all part of the fun … If, on the other hand, I had assembled the new models well enough to be put on display, I tied lengths of cotton thread to the wings and fuselage and suspended my treasures from the bedroom ceiling.[58]

Of course, the smell of burning polystyrene that Ward remembers fondly was a mere whiff of the fallout threatened by flying objects during the Cold War. 'Mutual assured destruction' was the haunting mainstay of nuclear missile development, and civil panic waxed and waned over the 1950s and 1960s, brought to a head by moments such as the Cuban Missile Crisis in October 1962. Tests were conducted in remote parts of the world until a treaty limiting them to underground sites was signed in 1963. Though nuclear weapons were not used in the Korean or Vietnam wars, these conflicts brought new USSR and US jet fighters into combat. North Korea was comprehensively carpet bombed by the US Air Force in 1950, with few

Copyright photograph by permission of Imperial War Museum.

Just like the real thing

Airfix kits are not just models—they're exact replicas, each series to a constant scale.

There are models galore in the Airfix range! Aircraft from fighters to bombers (*all* to the same 1/72nd scale), 00 gauge railway accessories, vintage cars, warships. Airfix value is *unbeatable*— ask your dealer for the latest list.

Airfix 1/72nd scale Lancaster bomber, 17" wing span. 7/6d.

Nearly 100 kits from 2/- to 10/6.

AIRFIX

THE WORLD'S GREATEST VALUE IN CONSTRUCTION KITS

From Model and Hobby Shops, Toy Shops and F. W. Woolworth

TRACKSIDE SERIES
Level Crossing 2/-

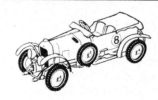

VINTAGE CARS
1930 Bentley 2/-

MODEL FIGURES
Lifeguard 2/-

HISTORICAL SHIPS

large buildings left standing. North Vietnam was devastated by even more American bombs in the mid 1960s.

With the rise in passenger aviation came a new phenomenon, hijacking. From the early 1960s commercial flights began to fall prey to passengers who smuggled weapons on board with ease, or who bluffed their way to intimidation with nothing more than a can of fly spray and a paring knife. Political activists saw the forced diversion of a flight as a high-visibility statement, and sometimes took hostages in exchange for the fulfilment of their demands. From the late 1960s there was a phenomenal number of 'skyjackings' in the United States by disaffected Americans demanding to be flown to Cuba.

In Britain several high-profile new aircraft contracts were cancelled by Harold Wilson's government in the mid 1960s in an attempt to shift spending to the welfare state. There was acrimony between procurement departments and manufacturers, and a sense that the country had had its day as a world-class aeroplane producer, with both the military air services and the national carriers depending instead on American aircraft. Restructuring in the RAF added to the sense that Britain's glory days were behind it. As the fiftieth anniversary of the founding of the RAF approached and it became apparent that the government would not fund a celebratory air display, one officer decided to exercise an astonishing act of nonconformity. On 5 April 1968 Flight Lieutenant Alan Pollock made a completely unscheduled demonstration flight over London in a jet-powered Hawker Hunter. He circled Westminster three times, making such a noise that the debate in the House of Commons had to be halted, then tilted his wings in salute to the RAF Memorial on the nearby Westminster Embankment, set off eastwards along the river and flew under the top walkway of Tower Bridge, which was full of the usual road traffic. Pollock also buzzed several airfields on this impromptu glory lap before landing at his West Raynham base and being arrested, never to fly in uniform again.

It was the first time a jet had performed a stunt at Tower Bridge and Pollock's flight certainly made an impact. 'It did me – and a lot of other people – a world of good', one woman wrote to the *Daily Express*. 'I shall always remember the feeling of pride as I thought of that chap in control of so much power, and it revived memories of those wonderful fellows who during the war fought for our survival.'[59] The opprobrium of the Air Ministry and Pollock's RAF superiors prevailed over any spirit of triumph and nostalgia awakened in Londoners that day, and he was invalided out

... this should come as no surprise ➤ BOAC

BOAC Concorde advertisement, c.1969. In fact Concorde would only fly passenger services in British Airways livery, after BOAC and BEA were merged in 1972.

of the service to deny him the opportunity of grandstanding in a court martial about the state of British aviation. The maverick, daredevil ideal of the pilot, which had entered the national imagination with the First World War, was no longer encouraged. A few months after Pollock's famous flight the creator of Biggles, William Johns, died.

It was in some sense the end of an era for Britain, even if it had been a short one. The conclusion of a quarter century of aircraft manufacturing success was approaching. British companies continued to make engines and components for aeroplanes but, without the generous investment of post-war research and development, could no longer design and make new aircraft. One more huge project was in the pipeline: Concorde. This Anglo-French supersonic airliner, constructed in the second half of the 1960s, made its first flight in 1969 and offered its first passenger service in 1976. Though it went inordinately over budget, Concorde did attract fascination (and disgust) from those on the ground who could not afford its tremendously expensive seats. The sonic boom and loud engine noise were the subject of many complaints in England and France, and the United States banned it from flying over its territories on the grounds of public disturbance. A source of national pride and a pleasing product of collaboration between the two old rivals of Britain and France, it flew between the two countries and the eastern seaboard of the United States for twenty-seven years.

The small island nation, so determined to rule the air as it had ruled the waves, had lost control of its military aircraft production and been divested of the empire that justified large airline subsidies. Britain did not have the skills or spending power to compete in the space race, the new arena for national technological prowess. And yet this was the moment when flight was at last becoming much more widely accessible. Boeing 747s transported one million paying passengers in their first six months of operations in 1970. British holiday-makers were increasingly able to travel abroad in the 1970s, a phenomenon that has continued to the present day.

By the end of the 1960s flight was no longer a dream, and soon it would no longer be an inaccessible luxury either. Yet it retained elements of fantasy, from the patriot's nostalgia for Britain's fleeting air supremacy to the jaded traveller's yearning for a more exclusive flying experience. And the conviction that powered flight would facilitate trips to the moon only became stronger after Sputnik bleeped its way around the earth in 1957. The oneiric quality of powered flight and its new limits were at no time more potent than in the early hours of 20 July 1969, when children were scooped out of bed to witness two Americans stepping onto the surface of the moon on live television. The moon walk, which prompted the BBC to run its first ever overnight programming, was watched by 530 million people around the world. The American songwriter Bart Howard had composed 'In other words' in 1954, echoing the lyrical tradition of romantic interplanetary excursions already seen in this book (Chapter 4). It was a popular song, better known as 'Fly me to the Moon', by the time Frank Sinatra covered it in 1964. Sinatra's recording with Count Basie, arranged by Quincy Jones, was adopted by NASA and, sure enough, was flown to the moon and back on Apollo 11. Playing out to an audience of two as Neil Armstrong and Buzz Aldrin paced the moondust, it was a reminder of the importance of dreams of flight in achieving this milestone.

Рисунок И. СЕМЕНОВА.

Ю. А. ГАГАРИН:— Полет продолжается нормально. Состояние невесомости переношу хорошо.

КРОКОДИЛ

№ 11 (1625)   ГОД ИЗДАНИЯ 39-Й   20 АПРЕЛЯ 1961

ABOVE: Yuri Gagarin, celebrated on the cover of *Krokodil* magazine, 1961.
OPPOSITE: Buzz Aldrin on the moon, photographed by Neil Armstrong, 20 July 1969.
OVERLEAF: Cover of *Speedbird: The BOAC Magazine*, summer 1948.

Conclusion

A remote event transmitted by radio signals and then cathode rays into the domestic sphere, the 1969 moon landing marked a departure in the experience of flight, not only for the NASA team but also for spectators. But this and other NASA expeditions retained the register of suspense that was familiar from flight attempts throughout history; there was enough uncertainty about whether rockets would launch or explode to keep audiences tuned in live. As we have seen, the appeal of witnessing ascents lay as much in the expectation of disaster as in the hope of success. Mrs Graham's hazardous balloon launches drew crowds time after time in the 1850s. A century later 20,000 more spectators arrived at Farnborough the day after John Derry's fatal accident. Flight was about attempting the impossible, but it was also about failing to overcome boundaries, becoming hostage to human error, running foul of the laws of physics or mechanics, or just plain falling.

The fails and falls themselves were widely disseminated. It is Icarus, the failure, rather than Daedalus, the success, whose name is most closely connected with flight. Robert Cocking and Franz Reichelt became immortalized not for their modifications to parachute design but for the details of their deaths, seventy-five years apart. Amelia Earhart's disappearance in the Pacific in 1938 arguably kept her name alive for longer than if she had survived her round-the-world flight. Disasters make better copy than triumphs, as Harriet Quimby found after being the first woman to fly a plane across the English Channel in April 1912, the day after the *Titanic* sank.

Nevertheless the newspaper was aviation's friend in its early decades and, without the influence of Lord Northcliffe and his *Daily Mail* prizes, British aviation would have been far behind its European neighbours at the outbreak of the Great War. Pioneer balloonists had had to blow their own trumpet in self-published travelogues in the 1780s. By contrast the *Mail* printed a long hagiographic profile of Wilbur Wright with alacrity after his arrival in Europe, creating a profile of the new figure of the aviator. Print media also found itself exploring the fantasy side of flying, as when *The Times* reported the flight of the steam-powered Arial, or the *New York Sun* intentionally published aerial hoaxes. Sometimes editors could not fail to be inspired by the naysaying of fiction writers, venting their fears about the world's major cities being laid waste 'before breakfast'. H. G. Wells had a lot to answer for.

From the nineteenth century the possibilities of participating in flight broadened, first through greater-capacity balloons tethered to entertainment hubs and then, after the First World War, through joyriding operations. One still had to be rich to have control over one's method of ascension, whether by balloon, airship or aeroplane, but for everybody else a taste of the upper air was available for a small price. The figure of the passenger took on more importance when airlines became part of the national story, and it was only at this point that women were encouraged into the air, to neutralize fears of risk and discomfort.

This shift in focus on the aeroplane, from sport or combat to transport, coincided with a reframing of establishment attitudes towards popular participation in flight. Whereas in the nineteenth century entertainment ballooning had been frowned upon, with men of science and even 1920s historians tut-tutting at the way aeronautics had been defiled by mountebanks, soon after the First World War even the government could see the utility of a population interested in aeroplanes. Air-mindedness was a virtue, though it was always linked to the bellicose circumstances of its conception (probably in an early meeting of the Aerial League of the British Empire in 1909). An air-minded nation was more likely to win wars, and therefore any engagement with flight was to be encouraged. Alan Cobham's flying circuses and the RAF's aerial displays, with their slapstick acting and thrilling stunts, were conducted in the strictest spirit of patriotism.

Participation in flight was not limited to taking a joyride or a scheduled flight. People queued up to test their piloting skills at exhibitions. They had their portraits taken in cardboard cockpits. They watched aviation films and read *Biggles* novels. They made aeroplanes in home workshops and in factories. Parallel with the impressive production quotas of icons of mid-century British aviation – the Gipsy Moth, the Spitfire and the Comet – were thousands of miniature replicas reproduced by an army of enthusiastic modellers. Britons could take to the air without leaving the ground.

Though it shaped the complexion and specificities of the history of flight, the technology that enabled it is not the only story. The dream of flying, the persistent ambitions and delusions around what flight might allow and the expectations and realities of feeling oneself airborne, were also factors in how balloons and then aeroplanes were developed, performed and received. The pilot and writer William Langewiesche suggested that the philosophical implications of flight were only beginning to be processed in his 1998 essay 'The View from Above': 'After a century of flying, we still live at a moment of emergence like that experienced by creatures first escaping from the sea. For us the emergence has been given meaning because we can think about it, and can perhaps understand the nature of our liberation'.[60] We may only have had 110 years of powered aviation but, as this book has shown, humankind left the earth both imaginatively and physically many times over the last two millennia. The cultures of flight accumulated over that time tempered twentieth-century aviation and will, in turn, affect the ambitions and modes of flight that are developed in the present century. As Langewiesche has remarked, 'Mechanical wings allow us to fly, but it is with our minds that we make the sky ours'.[61]

Notes

1   Robert Wohl, *A Passion for Wings: Aviation and the Western Imagination*, 1908–1918 (New Haven: Yale University Press, 1994) and *The Spectacle of Flight: Aviation and the Western Imagination*, 1920–1950 (New Haven: Yale University Press, 2005).

2   Quoted in David Edgerton, *England and the Aeroplane: Militarism, Modernity and Machines*, rev. edn (1991; London: Penguin, 2013), p. 170.

3   Quoted in Bayla Singer, *Like Sex with Gods: An Unorthodox History of Flying* (College Station: Texas A&M University Press, 2003), p. 61.

4   *An Ottoman Traveller: Selections from the 'Book of Travels' by Evliya Çelebi*, translated with commentary by Robert Dankoff and Sooyong Kim (London: Eland 2010), p. 30.

5   Quoted in Marjorie Hope Nicolson, *Voyages to the Moon* (New York: Macmillan, 1960), p. 34.

6   John Wilkins, *Mathematicall Magick* (London: printed by M[iles]. F[lesher]. for Sa: Gellibrand at the brasen Serpent in Pauls Church-yard., 1648), p. 200.

7   Quoted in Marjorie Hope Nicolson, *Voyages to the Moon* (New York: Macmillan, 1960), p.171.

8   See Viktoria Tkaczyk, 'Ready for Takeoff', *Cabinet* 27 (Fall 2007), http://www.cabinetmagazine. org/issues/27/tkacsyk.php [accessed 11/01/18].

9   Quoted in Marjorie Hope Nicolson, *Voyages to the Moon* (New York: Macmillan, 1960), p. 122.

10 Charles H. Gibbs-Smith, *Aviation: an historical survey from its origins to the end of the Second World War* (London: Science Museum, 2003 [first published 1985]), p. 30.

11 *The Works of Thomas Carlyle*, Vol. II: *The French Revolution: A History*, ed. Henry Duff Trail (Cambridge: Cambridge University Press, 2010), p. 51.

12 Ibid.

13 Quoted in Eric Hodgins and F. Alexander Magoun, *Sky High: The Story of Aviation* (Boston: Little, Brown, 1929), p. 23.

14 Quoted in Richard Holmes, *Falling Upwards: How We Took to the Air* (London: William Collins, 2013), pp. 17–18.

15 John Jeffries, *A Narrative of the Two Voyages of Dr Jeffries with Mons. Blanchard, with Meteorological Observations and Remarks* (London: J. Robson, 1786), p. 12.

16 Letter to Faujas de St. Fond quoted in *The New Monthly Magazine* 48 (1836), p. 57.

17 H. G. Wells *The War in the Air and particularly how Mr. Bert Smallways fared while it lasted* (London: George Bell and Sons, 1908), p. 68.

18 Poster of the first Aeronautical Exhibition reproduced in John E. Hodgson, *The History of Aeronautics in Great Britain, from the earliest time to the latter half of the nineteenth century* (London: Humphrey Milford, 1924), p. 283.

19   Thomas Monck Mason, *Aeronautica; or, Sketches Illustrative of the Theory and Practice of Aero-station* (London: F. C. Westley. Repr. 1972. Richmond, Surrey: The Richmond Publishing Co, 1838), p. 245.

20   See Richard Holmes, *Falling Upwards: How We Took to the Air* (London: William Collins, 2013).

21   Quoted in David W. Wragg, *Flight before Flying* (Reading: Osprey, 1974), p. 26.

22   Quoted in Alexander Fraser, *The Balloon Factory: The story of the men who built Britain's first flying machines* (London: Picador, 2011), p. 30.

23   'The Aerial Ship! or A Flight of Fancy' (1843).

24   'Oh What Fun: A Comic Song' (1843).

25   'In Nineteen Hundred and Three', written and composed by C. M. Lea (New York: Willis Woodward; London: Charles Sheard, 1894).

26   *New York Herald*, February 1909, quoted at http://www.wrightstories.com/afterwards.html [accessed 29/08/17].

27   Quoted in Robert Wohl, *A Passion for Wings: Aviation and the Western Imagination, 1908–1918* (New Haven: Yale University Press, 1994), p. 113.

28   André Beaumont, *My Three Big Flights* (London: Eveleigh Nash, 1912), p. 42.

29   Harald Penrose, *British Aviation: The Pioneer Years 1903–1914* (London: Cassell, 1980), p. 28.

30   Quoted in Peter Adey, *Aerial Life: Spaces, Mobilities, Affects* (Chichester: Wiley-Blackwell, 2010), p. 56.

31   'Britannia Must Rule the Air', written by Frank Duprée, composed by Charles Ashley (London: Lawrence Wright Music Co., 1913).

32   Hendon Air Display Programme, May 1913, quoted in Adey, *Aerial Life*, p. 58.

33   Michael Macdonagh, *In London during the Great War: The Diary of a Journalist* (London: Eyre & Spottiswoode, 1935), p. 131.

34   Macdonagh, *In London During the Great War*, p. 132.

35   Macdonagh, *In London during the Great War*, pp. 135–6.

36   Quoted in Patrick Deer, *Culture in Camouflage: War, Empire and Modern British Culture* (Oxford: Oxford University Press, 2009), p. 62.

37   Quoted in Nigel Steel and Peter Hart, *Tumult in the Clouds: The British Experience of the War in the Air, 1914–1918* (London: Hodder & Stoughton, 1997), pp. 244–5.

38   'Future Policy in the Air', speech transcribed in H. A. Jones, *The War in the Air: Being the Story of the Part Played in the Great War by the Royal Air Force*, vol. 2 (1928; London: Hamish Hamilton, 1969), p. 474.

39   Sir John Monash, quoted in Jerry Brown, *Zeppelin Nights: London in the First World War* (London: Bodley Head, 2014), p. 170.

40   Le Corbusier, *Aircraft* (London: The Studio, 1935), p. 8.

41   Quoted in Gordon Pirie, *Air Empire: British Imperial Civil Aviation 1919–39* (Manchester: Manchester University Press, 2009), p. 30.

42   Union Theatre advertisement, quoted in Robert Dixon, *Prosthetic Gods: Travel, Representation and Colonial Governance* (St Lucia: University of Queensland Press in association with API, 2001), p. 65.

43   Alan Cobham, *Skyways* (London: Nisbet, 1925), pp. 304–5.

44   Quoted in Colin Cruddas, *Those Fabulous Flying Years: Joy-Riding and Flying Circuses between the Wars* (Tunbridge Wells: Air-Britain, 2003), p. 32.

45   Peter Fritzsche, *A Nation of Fliers: German Aviation and the Popular Imagination* (Cambridge, MA: Harvard University Press, 1992), p. 199.

46   Quoted in Robert Wohl, *The Spectacle of Flight: Aviation and the Western Imagination, 1920–1950* (New Haven: Yale University Press, 2005), p. 67.

47 Bob Learmonth, Joanna Nash and Douglas Cluett, *Croydon Airport: The Great Days 1928–1939* (Sutton, Surrey: London Borough of Sutton Libraries and Arts Services, 1980), p. 43.

48 David Davies, 'An International Police Force', quoted in Waqar H. Zaidi, "Aviation Will Either Destroy or Save Our Civilization": Proposals for the International Control of Aviation, 1920–45', *Journal of Contemporary History* 46:1 (January 2011), pp. 150–78, p. 165.

49 *The Skybird* 1:1 (1933), p. 18.

50 *The Skybird* 1:4 (1934), p. 33; 1:2 (1934), p. 39.

51 Quoted in Robert Wohl, *The Spectacle of Flight: Aviation and the Western Imagination, 1920–1950* (New Haven: Yale University Press, 2005), p. 214.

52 Quoted in Daniel Swift, *Bomber County* (London: Hamish Hamilton, 2010), p. 141.

53 Quoted in Swift, *Bomber County*, p. 142.

54 R. J. Overy, *The Air War 1939–1945* (1980; London: Papermac, 1987), p. 126.

55 'Fly me to the Moon (In other words)', words and music by Bart Howard (New York: Almanac, 1954).

56 Igor Cassini in the *New York Times Magazine*, 28 October 1962, p. 32 (Oxford English Dictionary).

57 David Edgerton, *England and the Aeroplane: Militarism, Modernity and Machines* (1991; London: Penguin, 2013), pp. 156, 146, 143.

58 Arthur Ward, *Airfix: Celebrating 50 Years of the World's Greatest Plastic Kits* (London: Harper-Collins, 1999), p. 6.

59 Quoted in James Hamilton-Paterson, *Empire of the Clouds: When Britain's Aircraft Ruled the World* (London: Faber & Faber, 2010), p. 268.

60 William Langewiesche, *Aloft* (London: Penguin, 2010), p. 1.

61 Ibid.

Bibliography

Peter Adey, *Aerial Life: Spaces, Mobilities, Affects*. Oxford: Wiley-Blackwell, 2010.

Aeronautical Classics No. 1 (collection of nineteenth-century writings on flight including Cayley, Stringfellow and Pilcher). London: Royal Aeronautical Society, 1910.

Scott Anthony, 'The Future's in the Air: Imperial Airways and the British Documentary Film Movement'. *Journal of British Cinema and Television* 8:3 (2011), pp. 301–21.

Scott Anthony and Oliver Green, *British Aviation Posters: Art, Design and Flight*. Farnham: Lund Humphries in association with British Airways, 2012.

Tom Crouch, *Wings: A History of Aviation from Kites to the Space Age*. New York: Smithsonian National Air and Space Museum in association with W. W. Norton, 2003.

Colin Cruddas, *Those Fabulous Flying Years: Joy-Riding and Flying Circuses between the Wars*. Tunbridge Wells: Air-Britain, 2003.

Charles Dollfus and Henri Bouché, *Histoire de L'Aéronautique*. Paris: *L'Illustration*, 1932.

David Edgerton, *England and the Aeroplane: Militarism, Modernity and Machines*. (Revised edition) London: Penguin, 2013 (first published 1991).

Jeffrey A. Engel, *Cold War at 30,000 Feet: The Anglo-American Fight for Aviation Supremacy*. London: Harvard University Press, 2007.

Peter Fritzsche, *A Nation of Fliers: German Aviation and the Popular Imagination*. London: Harvard University Press, 1992.

Charles H. Gibbs-Smith, *Aviation: an historical survey from its origins to the end of the Second World*

War. London: Science Museum, 2003 (first published 1985).

Alfred Gollin, *No longer an island: Britain and the Wright Brothers: 1902–1909*. London: Heinemann, 1984.

Peter Haining, *The Dream Machines*. London: The New English Library, 1971.

Peter Haining, *The Compleat Birdman*. London: Robert Hale, 1976.

Richard Hallion, *Taking Flight: Inventing the Aerial Age, from Antiquity through the First World War*. New York: Oxford University Press, 2003.

Eric Hodgins and F. Alexander Magoun, *Sky High: The Story of Aviation*. Boston: Little, Brown 1929.

John E. Hodgson, *The History of Aeronautics in Great Britain, from the earliest time to the latter half of the nineteenth century*. London: Humphrey Milford, 1924.

Richard Holmes, *The Age of Wonder: how the Romantic generation discovered the beauty and terror of science*. London: HarperPress, 2008.

Richard Holmes, *Falling Upwards: How We Took to the Air*. London: William Collins, 2013.

Andrew Horrall, *Popular Culture in London, c. 1890–1918: The Transformation of Entertainment*. Manchester: Manchester University Press, 2001.

William Lockwood Marsh, *Aeronautical Prints and Drawings*. London: Halton and Truscott Smith Ltd, 1924.

Liz Millward, *Women in British Imperial Airspace, 1922–1937*. Montreal and London: McGill-Queen's University Press, 2008.

Marjorie Hope Nicolson, *Voyages to the Moon*. New York: Macmillan, 1960.

Richard J. Overy, *The Air War 1939–1945*. London: Papermac, 1987 (first published 1980).

David Pascoe, *Airspaces*. London: Reaktion, 2001.

Gordon Pirie, 'Cinema and British Aviation, 1919–1939', *Historical Journal of Film, Radio and Television*, 23:2 (2003) pp. 117–31.

Gordon Pirie, *Air Empire: British imperial civil aviation, 1919–39*. Manchester: Manchester University Press, 2009.

L. T. C. Rolt, *The Balloonists: the history of the first aeronauts*. Stroud: Sutton, 2006 (first published 1966).

Bayla Singer, *Like Sex with Gods: an unorthodox history of flying*. College Station, Texas: Texas A&M University Press, 2003.

Adrian Smith, 'The Dawn of the Jet Age in Austerity Britain: David Lean's *The Sound Barrier* (1952)', *Historical Journal of Film, Radio and Television* 30:4 (2010), pp. 487–514.

Arthur Ward, *Airfix: celebrating 50 years of the world's greatest plastic kits*. London: HarperCollins, 1999.

Robert Wohl, *A Passion for Wings: Aviation and the Western Imagination, 1908–1918*. New Haven and London: Yale University Press, 1994.

Robert Wohl, *The Spectacle of Flight: Aviation and the Western Imagination, 1920–1950*. New Haven and London: Yale University Press, 2005.

David W. Wragg, *Flight before Flying*. Reading, UK: Osprey, 1974.

Sharon Wright, *Balloonomania Belles: Daredevil Divas Who First Took to the Sky*. Barnsley: Pen and Sword, 2018.

Other resources

Bella C. Landauer Collection of Aeronautical Sheet Music, Smithsonian Libraries:
www.sil.si.edu/ondisplay/Music/
British Pathé online archive: www.britishpathe.com
Flight Gallery, Science Museum, London.

Picture Credits

Index